# The
# FACE
## of
## Expression
## 2

*AARON WOODSON*

TaylorMade Publishing

www.TaylorMadePublishingFL.com
Jacksonville, FL 32218
904-323-1334

**The FACE of Expression 2: In your Face**
© 2020 Aaron Woodson
ISBN# 978-0-9968123-6-8

All rights reserved.

This book or parts of thereof may not be reproduced in any form, stored in a retrieval system, or transmitted in any form by an y means; electronic, mechanical, photocopy, recording, or otherwise without prior written permission of the publisher or author, except as provided by United States of America copyright.

Published by TaylorMade Publishing, May 2020
www.TaylorMadePublishingFL.com

# Contents

DEDICATION ............................................................................................. i
   Life & Military ................................................................................. 1
A LETTER TO MY MOM ........................................................................ 2
HOME SWEET VALLEJO ...................................................................... 3
BLACK BOY JOY .................................................................................... 4
DISCOVERING MY TRIBE .................................................................... 5
COLOR-BLIND ....................................................................................... 6
HOME OF THE BRAVE (OPERATION INHERENT RESOLVE) ........ 7
BLACK CONSCIENCE ........................................................................... 8
PANCAKES .............................................................................................. 9
88 KEYS (Tribute to Granny a.k.a. Mrs. Fannie Wallace) ............... 10
RIGHT TRACK ...................................................................................... 12
THE BOUNCE BACK IS MY CLAPBACK ......................................... 13
ABANDON ............................................................................................. 14
MIRRORS AND SHADOWS ............................................................... 15
GHOSTBUSTERS ................................................................................. 16
THE BEST MAN I CAN BE ................................................................. 18
I NEED SOME ROOM ......................................................................... 20
FROM NOTHING TO SOMETHING ................................................. 22
DEAR SOLDIER .................................................................................... 23
LIFE IN IRAQ ........................................................................................ 25
GONE BUT NOT FORGOTTEN ........................................................ 28
ASHY ...................................................................................................... 29
REAL FRIENDS .................................................................................... 30
MY GRIEF ............................................................................................. 32
FOREIGNER (Muslim in US/American in the Middle East) ......... 33
CRITICIZER .......................................................................................... 35
   Romance ........................................................................................ 36
KARMA .................................................................................................. 37
WE ARE ONE: "MIND, BODY, HEART & SOUL" ............................ 38
ABOUT LAST NIGHT .......................................................................... 39
KEEP IT GOING ................................................................................... 40
MORE LOVE TO SHOW ..................................................................... 41

| | |
|---|---|
| I HAVE A BOTTLE | 42 |
| CATERERS OF LOVE | 43 |
| CONFETTI OF KINDNESS | 45 |
| POETRY | 47 |
| OH, WHAT A NIGHT | 48 |
| YOUR THOUGHTS | 49 |
| CLICK | 51 |
| ROMANCE AT ITS FINEST | 52 |
| BEST STORY THAT'S EVER BEEN TOLD | 53 |
| HORSES RUN FREE | 54 |
| UNAPOLOGETIC LOVER | 55 |
| TOO GOOD TO PASS UP | 57 |
| ECHO OF LOVE | 59 |
| SHOTS FIRED | 60 |
| ERUPTION | 61 |
| RADAR | 62 |
| PERSPECTIVES OF LOVE | 63 |
| WHAT IS LOVE? | 67 |
| YOU'RE MY FIRST LOVE | 68 |
| LOVE STILL MATTERS | 69 |
| DANCING PARTNERS | 70 |
| PATTERNS OF SEXY | 73 |
| BY FAITH | 75 |
| YOU JUST GOT SERVED | 77 |
| IT'S A DONE DEAL | 78 |
| I KNOW MY WORTH | 79 |
| SUNFLOWER | 82 |
| INTRIGUING LOVE | 83 |
| LOVE SONG | 85 |
| RING MY BELL/SOUND THE ALARM | 86 |
| SUMMER DRESSES | 87 |
| DOWNLOADED | 89 |
| TRAMPOLINE | 90 |
| IT'S TIME THAT WE SPEAK | 91 |
| MISSED OPPORTUNITY | 93 |
| LADIES ONLY | 94 |
| NEW NARRATIVE | 96 |

| | |
|---|---|
| HUMILIATION | 97 |
| RESTING BITCH FACE | 99 |

### God & Self-Improvement .................................................. 100

| | |
|---|---|
| DEAD TO THE WORLD | 101 |
| BRIGHT SIDE | 102 |
| BABIES THAT LEARNED HOW TO LOVE | 103 |
| PLAY YOUR POSITION | 105 |
| RISK-TAKER | 106 |
| WHAT MY FATHERS MEAN TO ME | 108 |
| INFLUENCE | 109 |
| THICK SKIN | 110 |
| EPIPHANY | 111 |
| INTERRUPTIONS | 112 |
| DEALING WITH MYSELF | 113 |
| SPEAKING MY PIECE | 114 |
| LITTLE BOY | 115 |
| A DEMONSTRATION OF LOVE | 116 |
| KEEP THAT SAME ENERGY | 117 |
| NO MORE RIVALRIES | 119 |
| BALANCE | 120 |
| INSPIRATION | 122 |
| NEVER LOSE THAT SMILE | 123 |
| GRUDGES | 124 |
| EXCUSES | 125 |
| TAKE ONE FOR THE TEAM | 126 |
| HE WILL CARRY ME THROUGH | 127 |
| MY ROAD TO DAMASCUS | 128 |
| THE CROSS | 129 |
| HUMAN TRAFFICKING | 130 |
| THE BLESSING IS IN THE WRESTLING | 131 |
| FACE YOURSELF | 132 |
| MAKE IT STOP | 134 |
| THE DAWN OF ENLIGHTENMENT | 135 |
| A MATTER OF PRECIOUS TIME | 136 |
| LORD, BRING US BACK | 137 |
| THE OVERCOMER WHO IS REDEEMED | 138 |
| TIME'S UP | 139 |

| | |
|---|---|
| CLOUT CHASER | 141 |
| THE THRONE | 142 |
| PHOBIAS | 143 |
| ANXIETY | 145 |
| BREAKING BARRIERS | 146 |
| TRANSITION | 147 |
| L.G.B.T. (LET GOD BRING TRUTH) | 149 |
| GIFT OF PRAISE | 151 |
| FOR THE WIDOWS | 152 |
| ROBBED | 154 |
| SERVING GOD'S PEOPLE | 156 |
| SELF-CARE | 158 |
| YOU MADE IT | 159 |
| MY JOURNEY: FROM THE MARATHON TO THE MOUNTAINTOP | 160 |
| ENCOURAGING WORDS FOR MY PEOPLE | 161 |
| LEARNING CURVE | 163 |
| KISS FROM GOD | 164 |
| FISHERS OF MEN (A FATHER & SON COLLABORATION) | 165 |
|    Emcee Battles | 168 |
| RESPECT IT | 169 |
| ALL UP IN YOUR SPACE | 170 |
| I CARRY WEIGHT | 171 |
| I'M THE MAN | 173 |
| JEALOUSY | 174 |
| COMING OUT THE FRAME | 175 |
| DON'T POKE THE BEAR | 176 |
| RESPECT MY CALIBER | 177 |
| HE DID IT | 178 |
| GENIUS IS COMMON | 179 |
|    About the Author | 180 |

# DEDICATION

First and foremost, I want to truly give a special thanks to my LORD and Savior, Jesus Christ, who is the Head of my life. Without Him blessing me with my talent and gift to write, none of this would be possible. I also want to thank my parents, Robert Woodson and Shirley Wallace, for raising me to be the man I am today. I love you both dearly, and I always want to honor you and make you proud. To my grandparents, Ernest Wallace, Fannie Wallace, Frances Woodson and LeRoy Woodson Sr., you all are a blessing to me and I love you all so much. I'll never forget the lessons you taught me in life, especially teaching me to keep God first in my life. I honor you. Rest in peace and power! I'll see you when I get there. To my baby sister, Angel, keep believing and share light and love with people around you. I'm proud to be your brother, and I'm glad you're my sister. This book is dedicated to my family in California; my hometown of Vallejo, California; my friends worldwide; young kids, poets, artists all over; and those who are looking to be inspired. Special thanks to the FSTV Media Group, Jessica Hatch and Frizella Taylor of TaylorMade Publishing LLC of Florida. I thank you all for your contributions, and I'm very happy to have worked with you on this special project. Please enjoy this book!

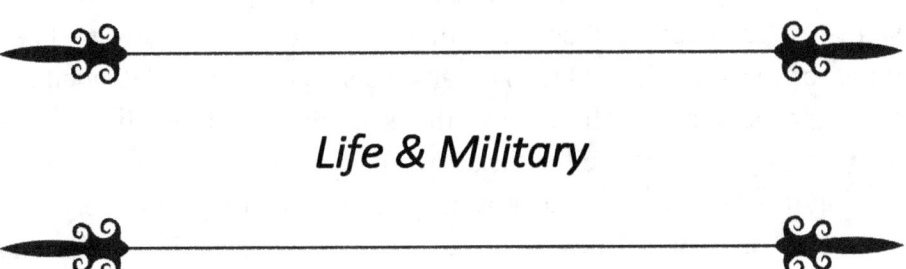
*Life & Military*

# A LETTER TO MY MOM

By Aaron Woodson

There is absolutely no one in the world like you! You carried me for nine months in your womb. We bonded while you were pregnant, and we finally got to meet face to face when you pushed me out—or should I say when the doctors cut open your stomach to get me out. Yeah, I was what they called a C-section baby. Nonetheless, I arrived on the scene and was very happy and healthy. I may have been a gift to you, but you were just as much of a special gift to me too. You've always been there for me since Day One. You always supported and defended me from the beginning. There were times in my life I felt like I was losing, but you made me feel like a winner. It's hard for me not to cry writing this letter to you. I just want you to know I tried my very best to make you proud. I always loved seeing your beautiful smile and just wanted to make you laugh. Sometimes I watched you cry, but you always were a strong Black Queen. You sacrificed so much for me and my sister; we can never thank you enough. All I ever wanted to do was honor, love, and respect you. I love the heart you possess. You always made room for everyone, including me. When I felt lost, you always found me and showed me unconditional love. I am so thankful that you're still here and that I get to celebrate you! Writing this letter is so personal for me. You're my Why, the reason I push myself to be successful! But I realize now that I'm already successful because you prepared me very well to take on this world. I'm so glad that I got to share every special moment I possibly could with you. I love you, Mom, always and forever until the end of time.

# HOME SWEET VALLEJO

By Aaron Woodson

I was born and raised in a village known to many as area code 707, a.k.a. Vallejo. The City of Vallejo is on the waterfront in Solano County, California, in the San Francisco Bay Area. My roots began there. I attended many different elementary schools—Beverly Hills, John Davidson, Elsa Widenmann, Highland, and Steffan Manor. Soon after, I made the transitions to Franklin Jr. High and my alma mater, Vallejo High School. I faced some trials and tribulations, yet I wouldn't trade them for anything in the world. I met some of the greatest people in my life in my hometown. Being surrounded by appealing diversity, scenery, and culture for eighteen years made Vallejo home sweet home for me! I will always remember where it all started and where I came from. I bleed red, and I bleed Vallejo. The City of Vallejo continues to have a special place in my heart. I'll never forget Vallejo. I'm its native favorite son! I always look forward to coming back for visits. I truly miss Home Sweet Vallejo. It helped raise me into the man I am today, and I am forever grateful to my beloved city. I love you, Vallejo!

# BLACK BOY JOY

## By Aaron Woodson

I got something called Black Boy Joy! I wake up every day feeling blessed. I thank God for giving me another chance to see a new day. The sun greets me every time I rise. It's always been my dream to walk among the stars. Life is far from perfect, but I'm enjoying every moment and taking it all in. I inhale peace and exhale passion. Showing love has always been in fashion. Confidence is the best outfit you can ever wear! Garments can be torn, but His favor will always adorn me! I'm happier than I've ever been. I'm radiating Black Boy Joy. I'm the sparkle equivalent to Black Girl Magic! The devil can't steal my joy. My lips are filled with praise for my LORD! He receives my best and He blesses me every time. My steps are ordered, and I am in alignment with Him. God took great pride and joy in creating me; surely I must return the favor back to Him! He has been so good to me. I thank Him by smiling and being thankful for all He does in my life. He is the reason I have Black Boy Joy: it's like heaven to my soul!

# DISCOVERING MY TRIBE

## By Aaron Woodson

I live in a place known as the land of the free and home of the brave. A few times in my life I have left my sanctuary to go overseas! I've always been a wandering soul, searching for my long-lost tribe. I have my own personal connections, but at the same time I feel disconnected. The only way to describe it is an emptiness that only I could ever witness. I have a strong, beautiful, and proud lineage that dates back hundreds of years. I fear the notion of not knowing my identity or where my ancestors come from. I have a fervent desire, passion, and need to find the deepest roots of my culture. I enjoy learning about different cultures, but I can't allow myself to subscribe to any of them. I refuse to borrow hand-me-down traditions. My people endured some of the worst conditions throughout history. History books portray us in certain ways. Each generation has faced its fair share of difficulties and challenges. We rose to prominence, and for a time we ruled with dominance. We brought out style, rhythms, and influence from the motherland known as Africa! We could dance all night until the sun came up! We were born melanated. You see we aren't just a pigment of the world's imagination. My tribe was discovered and enslaved for over four hundred years! We wore shackles of pain and shame. They tried to erase us from the face of the earth. Little did they know we were born to rise and were made for greatness. We are a distinct people. We refuse to become extinct! I can't wait to discover my tribe and transcribe a new narrative. I belong to a tribe that is beautiful and unique. WE ARE BLACK!!!

# COLOR-BLIND

## By Aaron Woodson

Every time I color, I can't seem to stay inside the lines. Crayons of different colors come in a box. Each one is unique. I came out of the box and I'm able to think outside of it! People often put so many limitations on their imaginations. My attraction goes beyond the surface, it goes much deeper. I don't let the outside become a distraction. I concentrate on the heart's presentation. Pure joy brings me ultimate satisfaction. I refuse to live in a prison of fear and criticism. I live my life in abundance and I'm free to make my own decisions. Like Bobby Brown, it's my prerogative! Don't Color Me Badd... I just like to paint with all the colors of the wind. I'm cut from a different cloth, but that's how I was meant to be! I will always be outside the lines... because I'm color-blind!

# HOME OF THE BRAVE (OPERATION INHERENT RESOLVE)

## By Aaron Woodson

Spent these last seven months deployed... gotta thank the Lord I'm still employed. However, there were times I got annoyed, but other times I did my best to try and enjoy being out of my comfort zone. Living out of a bag and on a prayer, I knew what to expect... I've been through this many times before. The environment around me and my brothers and sisters in arms was hard to ignore. The routine of eating, working, sleeping, and working out at the gym became the new normal for us. We all came from different backgrounds and are so diverse. Here we are, all dispersed in this foreign land, away from our homeland and what we all knew so well. We all came here to the desert to answer our nation's call... we had a mission and we had an enemy that needed to be eliminated. Our strategy was very calculated yet very effective. Drones and gunships rained down hell on ISIS... our archnemesis! As a member of Security Forces, I had the great pleasure of guarding those aircraft that dropped those bombs on Daesh aka ISIS. Bringing the fight to our enemy, we continue our relentless assault to end terrorism once and for all.

# BLACK CONSCIENCE

By Aaron Woodson

It's dangerous to be a black man nowadays. Every day you wake up is a blessing, but there is no guarantee that you'll even survive the day or night. Dark clouds have followed us, and we are haunted by painful memories in this struggle.

Our own people kill each other for no apparent reason. This is an act of treason! So quick to betray our fellow kings and queens! And we damn sure are emotionally sensitive when we feel judged or wronged by society. Yet when it comes to our behavior, we become ignorant, calloused, reckless, and hypocritical!

Trying to cover up our offenses like a retouched tattoo! The hurt that lingers is like the ink that bleeds into the skin and stays there permanently. Only God can heal us and make us whole. I'm proud to be a black man and I'm proud of my heritage, but let me be clear, I am a man of God first and foremost. My heart cries out for my people. Stop what you're doing right now... let's make a change!

Let's make a difference! Most of you claim to be woke, but I think you're just daydreaming. I think we really need to wake up from this nightmare we've been experiencing for so long. It's true the government has us in their scope, but usually we are the very ones pulling the trigger. Blllllaaaatttt.... blllllaaaatttt! We've been hunted, and now we've turned into the hunters. Violence needs to be silenced.

Let your voice be your weapon... put down the gun. Let's have fun being united! Let's enjoy Black Love again! Oh, and for the record... this is just my black conscience speaking to all of you!

# PANCAKES

## By Aaron Woodson

I remember those wonderful Saturday mornings I'd always look forward to when my mom would be on the phone with my granny. My dear granny would invite me, my sister, and my mother over for breakfast. And guess what we had? Some of her famous pancakes fresh outta the kitchen. As soon as we walked through the garage door, we came into the kitchen where a sweet and inviting aroma greeted our nostrils! I always felt like I was in pancake heaven. Pancakes have always been my favorite breakfast meal. My eyes were open so wide with joy when I saw the stack of pancakes that were on my plate. The Aunt Jemima syrup smothered my pancakes with a glazed affection! I said my prayers at the table, and soon afterward those pancakes were in my belly. I didn't even bother putting on any jelly. As a young boy I had a very big appetite. I tried to devour almost everything in sight. My granny made the absolute best pancakes in the world. It was such a wonderful treat for me and my family. Granny made her pancakes with love, and I felt it too. I was always so delighted to enjoy those pancakes. They were "oh, so good to my soul." I was well fed, but sometimes those pancakes would be kind of heavy on my stomach, so it wouldn't be long that those pancakes would put me to bed. I slept it off and woke up waiting for the next time I'd ever have those pancakes again!

# 88 KEYS (Tribute to Granny a.k.a. Mrs. Fannie Wallace)

By Aaron Woodson

You were born on April 12, 1931. God put you on this earth for a season. You are one of the main reasons I'm here writing this poem to you right now! It's my great honor and privilege to show you nothing but unconditional love. You deserve flowers and so much more. I really hope you can smell them now... your life was a sweet fragrance to the world.

Oh, how I adore you, my dear, sweet granny. Fannie Mae Wallace, you made such a significant impact on the many lives you touched. You were and continue to be a blessing to everyone that ever loved and knew you. Years went by seemingly so expeditiously... the love I have for you can be seen through the many tears that will be shed for you. You always made everyone feel welcome in your glorious presence. You always were the brightest; no one could hold a candle to you. You made me believe in myself. You made everyone else believe in themselves too. You made believers out of all of us because God was the center of it all in your life!

If you were an instrument, I would say you're the grand piano. I remember I always heard you sing the most beautiful church hymns. You sang in the choir, but soon you'll be singing with the angels in heaven. You will receive your wings and reward for being a true and faithful servant of our LORD and Savior! We celebrate you, my dear granny; your journey is now coming to an end. We know you've been tired for quite some time. Now may you rest in His kingdom.

When I see a piano, I will try to play a song and think of you! You were eighty-eight years old... The piano has eighty-eight keys. I would say you left us with many chords of memories. You will forever be a timeless treasure. Your legacy will live on, and I will always cherish everything we shared together. Even in the pain you endured, your resilience was a stroke of genius. You flashed radiance and grace with such unique humility.

Be with the King, my dear, sweet granny. Your eighty-eight keys will be struck on a HIGH NOTE to glory! I can hear you singing now... "Jesus keeps me near the cross!" or "The angels keep watching over me!" You're on the wings of love, and soon you'll be flying high. I'll look up to find you in the sky as I play the eighty-eight keys for you and only you! I love you, Granny! Till we meet again...

# RIGHT TRACK

By Aaron Woodson

I'm starting to pick up some steam, chasing this dream of mine. The A train has left the station, but the funny thing is I've been in search of a station to call my own. Some days I feel like a complete train wreck. I'm surprised I haven't derailed and got off track. My late grandfather worked for a company called Southern Pacific. He was a hardworking man that was built for his profession. Although he lost his bout with cancer, his spirit is alive and well within me. He sowed a strong work ethic in me that is ironclad. I'm so glad that God got me this far. He keeps me going as I endure this life of mine. Goals I will reach, stars I will meet, dreams I will achieve because I believe. I won't be stopped unless my heart stops! Passion fuels me; I haven't run out of gas yet! I'm still going, catch me if you can!

# THE BOUNCE BACK IS MY CLAPBACK

(The End of My Military Career)
By Aaron Woodson

Two years ago I was shown the door. My heart dropped to the floor. Flashbacks replayed in my mind from when I took an oath and then I was sent packing. After all I did for them, how could they do that to me? It was a gut-wrenching blow and they made their terrible decision... they never saw my worth! I was only seen as a number. I thought I was a member of an exclusive club, but the organization I was once proud to serve cancelled my enrollment. Disappointment, discouragement, anger, and depression hung over me like a dark cloud of torment. It wasn't supposed to be this way. I wanted to retire and secure my legacy... guess it wasn't meant to be. God has another plan for me. Sometimes, I feel like the legendary Robert Frost poem "The Road Not Taken." I could have chosen another path, but I took the one less traveled by. Now the path I take is uncertain, so I call this road "The Lonely Road of Faith." It would be much easier to go back to the familiar road; however, it would be nothing more than bittersweet. I waited two years to write this. Now I have closure. I'm over my nightmares, and I'm living my dreams. Peace of mind is the theme. My story isn't over; my journey continues.

# ABANDON

## By Aaron Woodson

I was a member of a band that was called family, but sometimes bands just don't stay together! Sometimes I go hmmm... hmmm... hmmm... like Al Green! I always thought we oughta stay together, but that whole idea went overboard and abandoned ship! It's hard to come back to a broken record. I wish we were all on the same sheet of music and full of harmony. These words I write are like the sound of the blues. The thrill is gone, like the late B.B. King once said. I often feared these tears would come flowing down my face like a river. I already had my one last cry; this time, I'm all dried out. I'm all alone on this desert island. I always tried to find my way home, but no matter what it's never the same. I feel like a foreigner in my own backyard. I feel abandoned at times, but I know I abandoned my family too! I went off to serve my country many years ago and left my family behind. I made a choice to make a better life for myself. Little did I know, I would be introduced to trauma, growing pains, and life lessons. Some things left me a little shook, yet I still endured by the grace of God. I still progressed in spite of all my stress. I'm not looking for sympathy! I'm not a victim; I'm a man of truth that needs love and therapy!

# MIRRORS AND SHADOWS

By Aaron Woodson

Every day we have to look at ourselves in the mirror. We see the image reflecting back at us, reminding us of who we truly are. Mirrors don't lie. Whenever I stand in front of a mirror, I see the good, the not so good, and the potential of what I can become. Mirrors greet us and expose the real truth about ourselves. Mirrors are like a spotlight; it focuses on you! Whenever you step into the light, do you ever notice something following you? It never leaves your side, it's a constant companion. What I'm referring to is shadows... they are all around us by day and by night! Shadows are dark silhouettes that outline your body structure or surrounding objects. Shadows are almost always behind you or on the side of you. Shadows can represent your past that so many of us may want to leave behind. Sometimes we feel like we are in someone else's shadow. We may feel pressure to live up to the expectations of what those people set before us. Shadows have also been described about one's mortality or nearing the end of life. When I see my grandmother battling dementia, I can see clearly that she is only a shadow of her former self, but her spirit is so full of light and love! At some point we all will have to face this fate. We could even be battling our own shadows of fear... shadows of rejection... shadows of despair... shadows of doubt... shadows of abandonment... and more! You rarely see shadows in mirrors. Shadows can be intimidating and possibly haunt you. Mirrors look deep within. People you encounter will be your mirror or your shadow... know the difference!

# GHOSTBUSTERS

By Aaron Woodson

There are times that I post on Facebook and I share my story. I share certain aspects of my life. I share my heart. I'm quite transparent, but it's apparent that some people will read my posts and not show any love whatsoever. They become (ghosts). There's something strange in the Facebook community... Who you gonna call? GHOSTBUSTERS! Yes, I'm a ghostbuster, not to be confused with a ghostwriter! I'll ghost-ride the whip... but I ain't afraid of no ghost! My page is always welcome for people to browse through. I extend the invitation to greet my followers with refreshing, original, and inspiring material. The content that I post is read for some reason, which leads me to believe people want to know more about it or just be plain nosey. Maybe, just maybe, they might find me interesting. These days it's rare that people ask me anything about who I am. I ask people about themselves because I'm curious. We live in a world where people would rather read about you, gossip and talk circles around you, before they would want to engage in any conversation with you! There's no reason to be scared; I'm not out to hurt anyone. It's just kind of sad people may feel some type of way, but at the same time I'm glad that I'm getting noticed. We all are capable of causing hurt and damage, yet we are more than capable of so much more. We have the ability to express, receive, give, and release the power of love. We have access to each other, but we often put up blockades against each other to feel some sort of protection. Sounds like a boundary to me! I believe that for walls to come down, there has to be a sense of trust. Do they trust me? Do I trust me? Do I even trust you or them? I guess I'll find out one way or the other. Writing is one of my passions, so it's only natural that I advertise. So I advise my viewers and followers to pay close attention. I may speak a language you may not even comprehend, but it doesn't mean that it doesn't make sense. I write it and walk it like I talk it! I just want to be clear: don't appear just to disappear. That just screams out fear and cowardice! Be intentional and reject passivity! This is my classroom. I post on my blackboard or whiteboard about anything I choose to transcribe. You can choose to be present or absent from this curriculum! The choice is yours. Just remember, ghosting is strictly prohibited. Don't let this ghostbuster catch you or it's a wrap!

# THE BEST MAN I CAN BE

By Aaron Woodson

A baby crawls before it walks; a man falls but gets back up to keep pressing on! One thing after another... it just goes on and on. Everything stops except for time, been down to my last nickel and dime. Tough times don't last; tough people do. I've done my dirt and had to feel the hurt. Chasing all these skirts didn't do a damn thing for me. I lost one because of my stupidity. A relationship that was meant for longevity collapsed like crumbling pillars.

I didn't take care of the foundation; I was careless and irresponsible! Being without my rib is so incomprehensible, yet I got only myself to blame. Oh, what a shame. I thought I played the game to my advantage. Little did I realize that I was the fall guy known as the pawn on the chessboard. I took myself out of the game by being so arrogant and blind. I didn't know how to be a king even though I tried to act like one. I made it all about me when it should have really been about us.

As time passes by, I've struggled to forgive myself for these serious offenses I caused you. I had to look at the man in the mirror to find out my identity again. I have nothing to compare myself to except the reflection I see looking back at me. I don't like what I did to you, but damn it, I'm so much better than that! How can I make you see the man you once knew and loved? I'm not a monster, just a man who has been battling his demons. Maybe I deserve to lose everything, but I can't afford to lose what makes me whole.

We both are wounded, but I inflicted the most damage. It's time that we both heal. Please forgive me. I'm not expecting to be excused from my wrongdoing. I'm just asking you not to hold any grudges against me. I'm so sorry. I can't take anything back. I know I've lost trust, but what I've lost today, I hope I can get back someday. I admit my guilt, and I will have to answer to my judge. I just want to love you and do so much more for you and for us! It's all in God's hands now. Just know that I'm not the man I used to be... I'm better than before. I'm just trying to be the best man I can be!

# I NEED SOME ROOM

By Aaron Woodson

I need room to grow
I need room to breathe
I need time to be alone
I need my privacy
I need room for improvement
I need time to process
I need closure
I need room to release
I need room to fit in my clothes
I need room to explore
I need a room to lay my head down at night
I need room to cool off
I need room to digest my food
I need room in bed to stretch out
I need room in the shower
I need room in my car
I need room to fit inside her walls
I need room to learn
I need room for understanding
I need room for strength
I need room to give myself a reactionary gap
I need room for my protection
I need room for your protection
I need room to walk
I need a room to speak in
I need room to exercise my freedom
I need room to lead
I need room to be creative

I need room to have some fun
I need room to be who I am
I need room to be who I'm destined to be
I need some room for leniency
I need some room in my bank account to make some deposits
I need a war room to go and pray to God
I need room to change
Please don't take any offense, but I need my solitude right now. So if you will excuse me... I need you to give some room!

# FROM NOTHING TO SOMETHING

## By Aaron Woodson

I'm a day late and a dollar short. Rent's due, tank needs gas, bills keep piling up like a mountain. Gotta make some ends, but I keep running into a dead end. Trying to make ends meet, but my lifestyle and cash flow just don't run parallel. Like Pharrell, I be frontin' to all my friends that I got it like that. Truth is, I ain't never had it like that! Money stays on my brain. Ignorance is my insanity. Expenses rarely have extensions. When shit is due, it's due. My pockets are spent. LORD, please show me some signs that make dollars and cents. I never want to be resentful of my struggle. My decisions and choices got me where I am today. I'm all about that revenue. I need some residuals to come in. Being broke is like being habitually addicted to oppression. Can't sleep 'cause I fall into a deep depression. Each day is agonizing turmoil and stress, all because of money! Money is funny, but I can't even laugh this time. I do my best to crack a smile even though it's crooked. Sometimes I want to frown or better yet drown in my sorrows. Somehow I'm keeping afloat. I'm like a turd that refuses to be flushed down the toilet. Sometimes I know I ain't shit and I really know how to stink it up. What would smell even better is that money green... I'd wear that as my new fragrance every day! You won't ever see me down like this ever again. I'll become an empire. Damn right, I require a lot from myself! It's down to the wire; everything is on the line. I made it this far; I won't be denied. I will advance and rewrite the script... from nothing to something!

# DEAR SOLDIER

By Aaron Woodson

Dear Soldier,

It is an honor and privilege for me to write this letter to America's finest hero! From one veteran to another, I've been in your shoes. I know what it's like to be deployed to a combat zone in a foreign country. Who knows how long you will be gone? Six months to a year, maybe? I can totally imagine how it feels being away from your family,  especially during the holidays. Separation can be very difficult. You try to close the gap in distance by making phone calls and writing letters. You can't physically touch your spouse or children, so you have to send your love to them in creative ways. You count down the days to when you actually get to see them again. While you're deployed, you have your unit that is like your family, and you'll form a bond with them. You may feel like you're forgotten, but believe me, our country really appreciates your service and great sacrifice! I have the utmost respect for you and what you do. Hold on, good soldier. What you're experiencing right now will soon pass. Continue to focus on your mission. Be safe and keep your head on a swivel. Also, watch you and your unit's six! You're built for this because you're a warrior. God is watching over you all. He goes before you and has placed you upon His righteous right hand! We are praying for your safe return. Please, let me know if you need anything. I'd be more than happy to assist you and your unit with some care packages. I hope we can stay in touch, but I understand if you can't always talk. Mission first! Get your mind right and stay in the fight! God bless you! Salute.

Sincerely,

TSgt Aaron Woodson

# LIFE IN IRAQ

## By Aaron Woodson

Once upon a time in March 2003, while serving in the US Air Force, I was activated to deploy to Baghdad, Iraq. I was only nineteen years old. As a young airman based out of the 97th Security Forces Squadron from Altus AFB, Oklahoma, I had never been to a foreign country! I was a part of a thirteen-man squad, all brothers in arms that went on a mission known as Operation Iraqi Freedom. I remember taking a twenty-hour-plus plane ride to Saudi Arabia. We stopped there first to set up a bare base. When we got there we had our briefings and had to get acclimated to our new surroundings. This is where our new home would be for the next six months. We all got assigned to live in a tent among many other tents in an area known as Tent City. The heat was certainly on. Every day we did our best to endure the temperatures that reached over 120 degrees. We always had to hydrate and press on with the mission. My team stood watch on post for fourteen hours a day. We worked a schedule of four days on and one day off. On our only day off, the majority of us only wanted to sleep, eat chow, do laundry, and talk to our families or spouses on the phone. Tension was in the air, and we were greeted with random sandstorms. We didn't stay long in Saudi; we got diverted to another direction: Baghdad, Iraq! We flew through the combat zone, and I remember we had to brace ourselves for a special landing called "The Combat Drop."

This was seriously a scary landing. We all felt a sense of relief once we hit the tarmac! I remember we deplaned and got our briefing regarding Saddam International Airport, which later changed to Baghdad International Airport. I saw murals everywhere of the Iraqi dictator at the time, Saddam Hussein. He held power for almost twenty-five years. He oppressed and brutalized many people in his country. He did the same to neighboring countries like Iran and Kuwait as well. Our team along with many other coalition forces were called up during this wartime situation. The commander in chief and president at the time was George W. Bush. He gave the order to send troops to Iraq. Tensions were high in the region when we deployed; we all had to watch each other's backs! I barely was two years removed from graduating high school, and all of a sudden I found myself in a combat zone with people I don't really know. We learned to trust each other and work together as a team. We had no other choice. We were all young, but we were very well trained individuals willing to do whatever it took to accomplish the mission! I remember going back to Iraq a second time, just three and a half years later in 2006. This time I was selected to be a squad leader for my seven-man team. We came from the 36th SFS Squadron out of Andersen AFB, Guam. While in Iraq, we were tasked to assist with detainee operations. In other words, we had to watch over inmates who committed crimes in their native land. Looking at the detainees from first glance, they all looked like a sideshow! They wore yellow jumpsuits to distinguish who they were. I remember coming to work one day in June, and members of my team including me were searching detainees for contraband and weapons they could be carrying with them. It was a blisteringly hot day, and we were sweating our asses off! We worked very hard, too, and had to don all our appropriate gear! Suddenly we all heard a whistling noise that immediately got our attention. Instinctively, we all knew it was "INCOMING," and we hit the ground in the prone position. In the moment of confusion and uncertainty, we realized that it was a mortar attack. From that moment on, we donned our gear and expedited to the site where the mortar round hit. To our surprise, we got to the scene and saw the fence line wide open. The detainees had apparently busted out in panic or fear. Thank God there were no wounded

Americans or casualties, but to make a long story short, the Quick Response force responded and held the line. We ensured the safety of the detainees that were in need of help.

Life in Iraq was different.
Life in Iraq was really hot.
Life in Iraq was uncertain.
Life in Iraq was filled with conflict.
Life in Iraq is intense.

We had no idea what could have happened in Iraq, but thankfully my team from the 97th SFS Squadron made it out alive! I'll never forget the lives that were lost either. Life in Iraq was a risk. Life in Iraq was a sacrifice!

# GONE BUT NOT FORGOTTEN

### By Aaron Woodson

I still can't believe it's been close to a year since you've been gone. Trouble is I haven't really accepted it. Whenever I think about it, I draw a blank. My heart sank like the Titanic as I grew frantic over what had occurred. It was time for you to leave, but I wasn't ready for you to depart. After this tragedy, I sought sanctuary to heal my wounds. I thought I may find peace, but I never felt completely restored. Sometimes you may think all is buried, but somehow it rises almost miraculously out of the ashes. Even though I still remember, you make sure I don't forget. Big Papa, there is not a day that passes by when I don't think about you. There is no one that will come before or after you. There is a place etched in my heart where you are welcome to dwell forever. You are gone but never forgotten!

# ASHY

## By Aaron Woodson

Have you ever heard of the term "ashy"? This phrase has been coined by many people to describe someone with dry skin or dry patches. When you're ashy, your skin looks like it's covered in snow. I'm sure all of us have been ashy a time or two. Believe me, it happens! I've been ashy so many times I've lost count. The only cure for ashiness is lotion! When I'm ashy my skin looks like Frosty Mini Wheat cereal or Frosted Flakes. Ashiness is a common problem among the population, especially among the melanated people. To my understanding, if you take a shower and put no lotion on your body, you will end up being ashy as hell! But seriously, some of us can't help but be ashy—we were born this way! If you want your skin to look like Soul Glo, you must moisturize it. I don't like being ashy. It's offensive to me and probably to other people that observe my ashy tendencies. If your skin looks like a chalkboard, then it's time for self-care. Our skin cries out for aloe and water daily. Ashiness can cause itchiness. People can tell when you're ashy—it shows! You're not fooling anybody! Bathe and purify yourself in the lotions of Bath and Body Works! Let's abstain from ashiness by being ashy-free!

# REAL FRIENDS

By Aaron Woodson

Real friends... how many of us have them? Ones we can rely on, depend on, and ones that can be loyal to us. Real friends are a rare gem these days. Not everyone will like you for who you are. You may not even like or accept people for who they truly are. Before you can ask for real friends, you must ask if you're a real friend yourself. I've asked myself this question over and over again, and I have found out that I am indeed a real friend. I'm not perfect, but I do care about people. It's nice to be loved and embraced regardless of race, origin, color, gender, sexual orientation, or nationality. Real friends can be quite diverse. Sometimes I think people's values are in reverse. Not trying to judge... I just observe what's going on around me. People fail you, but real friends are there for you during times of adversity. They believe in you. They love you even when you're at your worst! Real friends make you feel like you matter. Real friends never gossip about you; they empower you and edify you in front of other people. If you're a real friend, you should do the same and all of the above for them too! Real friends give each other their flowers while they can still smell them. They will even cry with you. Real friends will be honest with you even when you're wrong. Real friends are tokens that should be valued and never taken for granted. Real friends pray for you! Real friends involve you in their circle of life. Real friends will apologize if they have offended their friend. Real friends go through battles together and sharpen each other as iron. Real friends don't quit on each other; they always encourage one another to carry on! Even when the war rages on, real friends are courageous enough to have each other's backs! Real friends are a blessing. Real friends should mean the world to you!

Keep it real, my friends... be solid and not whack! Stand in the gap for each other. Be true and faithful, my friends. To all my real friends, I thank you for who you truly are. I'm so grateful and blessed to have you in my life. I hope you feel the same about me. Thank God for real friends!

# MY GRIEF

By Aaron Woodson

People expect my grief to be brief or for me to pretend to move on like nothing ever happened! I need relief from this horrible pain I feel in the deepest bowels of my soul. It's taking more time than I realized to heal from this—if I'll even heal from this! I can't guarantee how I'll get through this. All I can do is hang onto the promises of God in the meantime. We live in a calloused world filled with insensitive people. I'm not saying everyone is like that, but a majority of them are. I don't know whose lost anyone close to them before, but let me tell you something: that shit hurts so bad! Let me have my moment of grief! Maybe one day, I'll be glad to get over it. Until then nobody should expect me to get over something so quickly when it just recently happened. This isn't a pity party. I'm just asking for a little bit of understanding, empathy, and respect. No words or actions will ever bring my loved ones back. I do appreciate the comforting words of encouragement. They are very kind and helpful. I know one day I'll see my loved ones again in heaven. Until then just let me grieve in my own way. My heart is pouring out what needs to be released from within. Ladies and gentlemen, this is my time of grief!

# FOREIGNER (Muslim in US/American in the Middle East)

## By Aaron Woodson

Once upon a time there was a man who lived in a foreign land. He was a visitor in a new place, yet he strangely felt right at home. The man realized he was brought to this location for a reason, perhaps to find out his true purpose in life. Or maybe this was just a brief stop on the journey to where he was bound to go! Traveling can teach you so many things about particular places. You can learn about the laws of the land, the culture, and even speak their native language. As a foreigner it would be wise to adapt to your new surroundings; the world we live in is so fast-paced, so we have to do our best to keep up with the changing times. I know what it's like to be a foreigner. I lived in a few countries during my military career in the US Air Force. I lived in South Korea, Kuwait, and Iraq, just to name a few. Most of the locals enjoyed meeting Americans like me, but others wanted no part of us. They definitely didn't give us any red carpet treatment, that's for sure. I felt like I was the farthest away from home. I was also at my most vulnerable. Life doesn't come with any guarantees, especially when you're involved in a war campaign doing your duty to serve your country. I had faith knowing that God would protect me and my fellow comrades, but the threat was always a concern. We had families we needed to come home to, and I thank God that He delivered us all home safely. Since we are on the subject of foreigners, what about the foreigners that live in the US? There is always a lot of talk about whether they should be legal and legitimate citizens in this country. I believe people from other countries come to America for a better way of life. We are very privileged and blessed to live in the land of the free and the home of the brave. If people want to come here, we can welcome them here under a few conditions of course. We have laws for a reason, and they must be carefully considered and followed. I know a few immigrants that have traveled here to live and achieve their hopes and dreams. For example, I worked with a Muslim man from a different background than me. I spoke with him and he told me some interesting things about him and his culture. I was intrigued by the information that he was giving to me. I am a big believer in diversity. Just because we all look different, come from different countries, backgrounds, religions, cultures, genders, or sex doesn't mean we can't respect each other as human beings. There are people that live in the US that have bad intentions that have done terrible things or said bad things. There are others who are good and upstanding individuals that only try to make the world a better place. No one in this world is perfect, but at the same time we need to be open to having conversations about our differences. It's so easy to judge one another without actually getting to know someone. Even if someone is a foreigner, alien, or strange to other people, doesn't mean we have to treat them with contempt and disrespect. Let's learn to live in peace with each other. Violence and hatred solve nothing! We are all neighbors on this earth. We have a great responsibility to not only take care of ourselves and families, but also of the neighbors in our communities as well. We may be labeled foreigners on earth, but in eternity we are citizens of heaven. Until then let's settle things in a civil manner and learn about each other. Let's do the right thing and love our neighbors the way we are supposed to. Invite your neighbors to come to the table, not as foreigners but as your brothers and sisters. Peace be unto you all!

# CRITICIZER

By Aaron Woodson

We've all at some point in our lives been the recipients of constructive criticism. The words we use to speak to someone can bring joy or harm. Words can disarm people who are unexpectedly met by them. They can put us at ease or on guard. Some criticism is acceptable, and other times it's totally uncalled for! Criticism isn't necessarily for the weak at heart. You need to have a bit of tough skin to endure it. Sometimes criticism can be beneficial and do us good every now and then. If you find yourself being criticized, just remember it's not the end of the world. It happens to the best of us. Some people criticize others to make themselves feel better about their own insecurities. Sometimes it reveals our very own insecurities. Take criticism with a grain of salt and use it as an opportunity to grow. I admit that I am a total criticizer at times. I don't mean to be, I always think I'm helping someone. I realize that I come with no filter. I can be a bit much sometimes. I'm a work in progress. If I'm honest, I would say I take most criticism well. However, I don't receive it well when I feel disrespected. Criticism has actually made me a better person, and it can help you to do the same. You are more than what you're perceived to be doing. All you have to do is rise above it! It's all good. Criticism won't kill you. It will only make you stronger!

*Romance*

# KARMA

## By Aaron Woodson

Her name is Karma. Somehow she became my attraction, and I had to be extra vigilant. Her cruel and malignant ways try to keep me twisted around her little finger! She makes her presence felt from time to time. She hovers around me like a dark cloud. She works in mysterious ways... I can't seem to wrap my head around her intentions. Sometimes she greets me with a warm embrace or good fortune. Other times she sends me a message or pays me back for all the bad shit I ever did. Sooner or later, we all have to come face to face with her. Karma is a bad muthafucka. If me and Karma slept in the same bed, she definitely would come out on top! OK, let me stop before I get myself into more trouble. Beware of Karma; she definitely will put a spell on you.

# WE ARE ONE: "MIND, BODY, HEART & SOUL"

By Aaron Woodson

Funny, how we would have been
What we should have been
What we could have been....

But here we go again... what's it gonna be this time?
Now or never, we may not ever get this chance again. Can't let this opportunity slip through our fingers. When I look into your eyes, I find myself lingering just to peek into your soul. Maybe even to lean a little closer and leave my mark on those pretty lips. When we kiss, we are in perfect harmony. We learn to play each other like instruments. Love is definitely in the air tonight. Don't you hear that echo? Baby, your beautiful falsetto has lifted me up to the ceiling like an ascension. Just wait until you see my descension. I'm ready to give you my full extension. I want to hear you call out my name. Say it like you mean it! We are so much in the mood right now. We're in the moment!

What would have been
What should have been
What could have been...
Is happening right now.

We have moved beyond the past. This love is gonna last. We are moving forward. We have started a new chapter: "WE ARE ONE: MIND, BODY, HEART & SOUL!"

# ABOUT LAST NIGHT

By Aaron Woodson

I was wearing this new cologne called "About Last Night." It had me really thinking about what I did last night. I've had many good nights, but this particular one sticks out in my mind the most. Let me tell you that last night I wore a black-silk, buttoned-up shirt with a nice pair of black slacks. I had on my favorite Stacy Adams dress shoes. Like Biggie, I was feelin' Gucci all the way down to my socks. My hair was cut so nice, showing off my trademark crisp fade. I was trying to decide what I wanted to do for the night, and finally my mind was made up. I decided I was going to stay home tonight. However I was expecting some company for the night. I was at my place of residence, and I spent some time making this fine dish that my lovely guest would truly appreciate. I don't cook or go all out too often, but I made this a memorable one. Let this one marinate on your brain while you are fast asleep. Goodnight, baby... I'll see you in the morning!

# KEEP IT GOING

### By Aaron Woodson

Baby, I just want to make one thing clear... tonight our love takes precedence. There won't be any other considerations. It's just you and me. I've made reservations for us. I am here for you. Like Prince, I know love is meant for two! Now tell me what you're gonna do. To hell with hesitation, let's focus on our sweet meditation. The mind can't deny what the body already knows. Let's get on with the show, shall we? May our lips commence with each touch of seduction. If we're not careful, there will soon be an eruption taking place in this room! But we don't even care, right, baby? We're enjoying this sultry love affair, arms wrapped around each other so tightly... there don't seem to be any signs of letting go! We just can't get enough of each other. This ride is like an exciting rollercoaster. Thrills like this always gets my head spinning. I especially delight in hearing your beautiful screams. You and me together is like a dream come true. I just love it when you call my name. There is no shame in gettin' freaky! This game we play can never seem to come to an end! We can go on like this forever. There's no stopping us; let's keep it going!

# MORE LOVE TO SHOW

### By Aaron Woodson

I taught her how to love
I taught her patience
I taught her pain
But little did she know how amazing she would turn out to be.

She taught me joy
She taught me compassion
She taught me how to open up and share my emotions
But little did I know she would make me become a better man.

We learned how to share time and space.
We often found ourselves standing face to face, always looking forward to one another's warm embrace.
We were made for each other.

We got through all four seasons each passing year!
We shared our deepest secrets and fears.
We traded our past lives for this moment and beyond together!
I'm so glad we found each other!

Thank God for the lessons of love!
We made it this far and we won't stop now.
We still got a ways to go... there's more room to grow!
More love to show!

# I HAVE A BOTTLE

By Aaron Woodson

I have a bottle of thoughts.
I have a bottle of fears.
I have a bottle of tears.
I poured them all out like a glass of wine.
People thought I was fine.

But I wasn't... left to my own devices I turned to what gave me comfort. So many sleepless nights tossin' and turnin'. I was yearnin' for some real affection. I was thirsty for your love, yet there wasn't a drop of it anywhere to be found.

I felt like a wanderer in the desert searching for a well to drink from. Water ran dry as did your love for me. Barrels of oil can make you rich... yet being with you would have made me the wealthiest man alive! You are worth more than silver or gold; your price is far above rubies.

I couldn't afford you, but I always knew I could love you better than anyone else. I would walk a thousand miles just to see you. There's nothing in this world I wouldn't do for you. So here I stand feeling lost, lonely, and hopeless...

Blood leaves stains, and scars remain. Even though I had to let it burn, there is still beauty in the ashes... And I will keep them in a bottle inside my heart forever!

# CATERERS OF LOVE

By La'Rhonda Felton & Aaron Woodson

Catering to my love
As I pour him a glass of wine
I feel the giddiness of a teenager
Because he gives me butterflies.
As he waits at the table
I know he's watching me,
But tonight I'm the server
And dinner is my treat.
He works very hard
And he makes sure to provide.
I need him to know he's special
And he's always on my mind,
So I've prepared his favorites
And I will cater to his needs.
My love belongs to him;
That's all he asks of me.
But I felt he needed a pick-me-up,
Just a small surprise.
He's been stressed lately.
I can see it in his eyes.
He won't feel that pressure at home.
Here, it's peaceful and serene.
In the world he fights for position,
But at home, he's king.
This is his castle.
Serving him pleases me.
After all, he should expect
Nothing less from his queen.                (La'Rhonda Felton)

She caters to my every need.
I feed off every morsel of love she gives me.
She pours the wine, but I light the fire!
She satisfies me like no other.
Whenever I have a lot on my plate,
she takes the pressure off me and gives me pleasures I like!
She is the wax to my candle.
I melt in her presence every time we meet.
I love to wait on her. I think it's about time to let her relax now.

She needs to get off her feet. It's my turn to be her server.
Tonight, whatever she wants she will get,
Courtesy of her favorite chocolate chef!
I prepare a hearty meal that she can't wait to taste.
I love how she takes each bite. She chews her food so divinely.
The smile on her face lets me know I did an excellent job.
Now I'm ready to take off her shoes and rub her feet.
I get down on my knees and caress each foot with my
sensual expertise. I make her very comfortable,
now she can just enjoy the moment!
The look in her eyes tells me she is turned on. I love how they roll in
the back of her head... she is completely mesmerized by my touch.
I'm the master of seduction and foreplay. I'm showing her
the right way a real man takes care of his woman!
We made reservations for each other, and it's been an unforgettable experience!
We started from scratch, and now we are here...
we are certified caterers of love!        (Aaron Woodson)

# CONFETTI OF KINDNESS

## By Aaron Woodson

Let's throw a party, the kind where we shower each other with kindness like confetti.
It's time to stop cutting each other down like a machete.
Our words should be sprinkled with salt, but we never want to throw any of that on a wound.
Words can cause infection. However, they also have the power to heal. I only want to speak words that come from my lips to drip like a honey-comb for my honey.
Life and death are in the power of the tongue.
Words can make you or break you. They can be deceiving or truthful. We have to discern the difference by deciphering what's real and what's fake. Words have nuclear capability... they can destroy a person's soul.
On the flip side, they can also be used for encouragement and inspiration! Words can sometimes be replaced by emoji's or just plain silence. But even silence can speak volumes.
If you have nothing nice to say, don't say it at all.
Be a welcomed presence rather than a meaningless distraction.
Engaging conversations can be an attraction to the opposite sex.
Wordplay and playful banter can increase levels of interest. I slip in jokes that I know she can handle. I can live with her infectious laugh as it gives me a triumphant smile. Her expression gives me excitement... I am confident she likes me because it's written all over her face. And it was all because I was kind to her.
I made her day. Trust me... she'll tell you how it all went down if you ask her.
The next time you speak to someone, try a little kindness.

Try a little tenderness. Try a little respect. It will take you further than you could ever imagine. Keep spreading the confetti of kindness... the party is only for the grown, kind, and sexy!

# POETRY

By Aaron Woodson

Your name is like poetry. I can't help but magnify the beautiful creation that stands before me. You're impossible to ignore. You're like a door that leads me to my destiny. I just have to find the key that unlocks the mysteries of your love. I'm ready to embrace the new phenomenon that allows me to be this state of euphoria. I sweat profusely thinking about our escapade of ecstasy. Our flirtatious banter leads to a sexy romp in a special, private place. We have such wild thoughts and we lose all control. I'm patrolling areas of your body that have yet to be discovered. I've uncovered all the evidence... the love we have made is now like a crime; somehow we bent a few rules. I think we may have broken a bed or two. So, about last night... I'll keep it in my memory forever. The scent we left will be so unforgettable! Oh, how I love the sweet smell of sex in the morning. Lying next to you, looking into innocent eyes that peer into my soul... I feel like I'm in a dream, but this time, this seems for real! I'm like your page, and you're the pen. Together we make poetry that is so harmonizing and mesmerizing! But if I'm honest, I'm drawing a blank... you were the one who wrote this. I was merely available for you to work this magic. It would be so tragic if our love ran out of ink. Let that sink. I'd rather if we kept this thing going on! Poetry lives on to be our enduring legacy!

# OH, WHAT A NIGHT

### By Aaron Woodson

Please smell the aroma of sweet romance. Come a little closer; let me have a taste of those pretty lips. I'm quite thirsty for you. We drown ourselves in each other's love. Ecstasy hits us like a waterfall. I got to let you in on a secret: I can't swim, but I can learn to cross the ocean for you... Come and park yourself on my dock. I'll be your harbor... Don't worry, I got you covered! Better yet, I can have you uncovered in a minute. You're a mystery I'd love to unravel. I'll travel to my favorite destinations across your body. You know I got everything mapped out. I'm trying to hit that sweet spot so you'll be tapped out! I believe you got me tapped out too! This is one for the books... a memorable bout indeed! Oh, what a night!

# YOUR THOUGHTS

By Aaron Woodson

I don't want to leave you alone with your thoughts. I'm afraid if I leave, you might do something to hurt yourself. I just want to be your human shield and protect you from the pain and attacks you face. We all go through things in life from time to time, sometimes we need somebody to lean on. Sometimes we need somebody to talk to. Like Prince, just call my name. Like The Jackson Five, I'll be there! I'm still the one.

And if by chance I'm no longer around, just know there is one that is greater and He always will be there for you. Jesus is on the main line if you need to talk to Him. He always has the time for you. I love you more than you could ever know, yet God loves you all the way down to your soul! Truth be told, if you ever leave me I'd never be the same. Let's pull it together and know nothing can ever stop you except you. I'll do whatever I can to help you carry on.

I don't want to leave you with these thoughts... these suicidal thoughts that consume the human existence. I can't let you drown in your sorrows. If I could reach up in the sky and borrow the stars, I'd give them all to you so you could have a better tomorrow. Stay for the night. Joy comes in the morning. I'm praying that you will see the light... Keep fighting and let's soldier on together! We fight from victory, not to victory!

If you are weary, just know I'm standing right beside you. I'll be a true friend till the end. If you're on your last rope, just remember you have God to hold on to. He won't ever let go of you. I might be losing my grip watching you slowly slipping away... please don't throw it all away. I'm begging you. Your suicidal thoughts are killin' you and me... don't take the easy way out. Let me show you THE WAY...

Yahweh is His name and He is coming to your rescue. He's got you! Cast your thoughts into the depths of the sea. Be the wave that keeps on rising!

# CLICK

### By Aaron Woodson

People I know will be anywhere and everywhere. They say they love you or care about you, but their actions say otherwise. A call here, a call there. A text here, a text there. You only come around here and there. You only want a connection with me because that's you're only way in. That's exactly it: you're looking for a way in. I'm convenient when you just so happen to want something from me, and when I don't have what you want, you do a disappearing act. I don't mind giving, but sometimes you have to reciprocate. Relationships can be a delicate situation... please don't complicate it that much more! I'm here, but you're not present. I'm calling you, but you don't respond or rarely pick up the phone. You can't adore someone you constantly ignore. I guess you get bored. I'm not here to entertain you. Go to a circus or comedy show if that is what you're looking for! My time is expensive and valuable. I refuse to waste it on people that don't appreciate my time. I got a million things I'd rather do, yet I made time for you. That was clearly a mistake on my part... never again! You're now disconnected. This number is no longer in service; please try your call again later. I can almost assure you that I'll never pick up the phone. I've hung up on you for the very last time.

# ROMANCE AT ITS FINEST

By Aaron Woodson

I always wanted to cross into your border and show you what I was about. I know you've come across men you could barely trust, but somehow I must make you see that I'm quite different. I want to reveal my credentials and have you identify my true character. You can verify this by testing me through this trial.

I know what I'm worth, and I would love to show you the diamond I see. You caught my eye; I can't deny that I want you so bad. Yes, I'm so thirsty; I've come a long way to get a taste of you. You alone can quench my desire... The fire is lit, let this passionate chemistry begin to ignite! In plain sight, I've seen a beautiful angel bless me in all her glory.

Our eyes connect and burn holes into each other's souls like infrared beams. Read my lips: "Come here! Come closer!" We are like magnets, we can't help but attract one another. As we explore different locations around each other's faces, we begin to mark our territory. We navigate to other regions... find ourselves enjoying each destination we find ourselves in. I'm sure neither of us really wants this to end any time soon.

Our hearts contain citizenships of love. Let us dwell there with peace and harmony. Let's enjoy the beautiful symphony that is being orchestrated by you and me. We make such beautiful music together... now the curtain must fall as we continue our show behind the scenes! We make Broadway look amateur... this grand tour started at the border and the finale has yet to be determined. Stay tuned for the next show!

# BEST STORY THAT'S EVER BEEN TOLD

By Aaron Woodson

All I do is let my pen talk... my favorite language is the one your body is speakin'. Girl, you got me thinkin'. I wouldn't mind spending forever and a day with you. Is that all right with you?

You can be my Mona Lisa; I'll be your Da Vinci and do you just right! We can take a first-class flight to the land of ecstasy... I don't mind taking a nosedive as long as it's on your landing strip. Baby, your hips don't lie... I can't deny that I'm on one! We can take over the night and enjoy a few sips. I just want to taste those pretty lips. You got me feeling a little thirsty. I gotta tip my hat to you... you get it from your mama! God bless the one that made ya!

Tell me baby, what's on your mind? I want to be like NASA and discover what's in your orbit. There's a strong gravity between us or maybe it could just be chemistry! Your beautiful eyes sparkle like millions of stars so intricately placed in the night sky. I could make a wish right now and realize you made it all come true. All my life it seems like I've been jumping through hoops to find that one. I felt like I was in a circus, but somehow we found some time to entertain each other with good conversation. Next thing you know we're having a ball! Girl, we can have it all. Thank God I gave you a call. I'm glad I can be the man in your hall of fame. If we never crossed paths, it would be a damn shame. So thankful I found someone like you! Divine appointment or divine intervention call it whatever you want, it was meant for us to be! Now we got this one in the books... it's the best story that's ever been told

# HORSES RUN FREE

By Aaron Woodson

Before we met, I was but a horse dwelling in a stable. On the exterior I exuded an assuring confidence and steady calmness... however, truthfully on the inside, I just wanted to run away to secure my freedom. Several times throughout my life, I've been reminded that the grass isn't always greener on the other side.

There may be some truth to that statement, but I need to find a greater pasture suitable for such a stallion as myself. I've always been a lone star, and I'm determined to find my way. Yet no one ever told me that I'd find my way to you. On that day the shadow of darkness met the enchanting beauty of light. The encounter stands out as one of the most precious moments in my life.

I know we just met, but I would have liked to hit the racetrack with you and run free, carelessly. I know you run like the wind and you have admirers chasing after you. I'm just glad you slowed down enough for me to get your attention. I don't want to be a distraction, yet I desire to be your main attraction. A fraction of a second is all I need to make you smile. My saddle is up, and baby, I need a rider.

# UNAPOLOGETIC LOVER

By Aaron Woodson

All I ever want to do is love,
But sometimes I love "too hard."
I've learned to give space.
To go at a slower pace.

I miss the times I don't get to see your face. Absence truly
does make the heart grow fonder. I wonder
if you're somewhere thinking about me like I am about you.
I'm built like a statue, but that doesn't mean my heart is made of stone!

In the left side of my chest is a fragile but strong
beating organ known as my heart.
I was given a heart to love.
It's hard to love, but at the same time
it's even harder not to love!

I know that probably doesn't make much sense.
So let me explain. Love in the beginning can be
scary. You get butterflies. Once you get through that,
you're more likely to become more comfortable with what
love has to offer.

Even when the one you love makes you upset...
it's almost like you have the softest spot for them in your heart.
You love them so much! Anyone that may have
hurt you in the past wouldn't have lasted past the ire of
your wrath. But something about this person is different...

her love hits me a little different. It almost feels like I'm off
balance, but when we are together we are rooted in the soil of love.
Forgiveness is a big part of love...it's not always
easy but very necessary! She reminds me daily of why I
never want to be single again. I enjoy her companionship.

I love what she stands for and I love her imperfections, and she loves
me just the way I am. How could I not love her?
Seriously. There is no denying that my love is strong...
since when did being in love become such a crime?

I see people all around me in love with each other all the time.
I should be able to enjoy that same experience!
No, I don't envy any of them. I'm just saying it's nice to have that
special person in your life. I know it's not always sunshine
and rainbows. I know it's not always roses. What I do know
is that I'll never be ashamed to love. Love is what I do.
Love is my business. Love is what I thrive upon! Love is
my best friend.

I'd find any excuse to be in love if I had to...
love is the truth and it's just such a beautiful blessing to
share it with the one you value most dearly. Love comes
from God himself... He came to love and He left His love
behind for all of us to enjoy!

I'm unapologetically wired to
love someone. I love God and His love flows through my
veins and spirit. I'll always love no matter what.
I'm an unapologetic lover.

# TOO GOOD TO PASS UP

By Aaron Woodson

I can't go a day without thinking about you. In my wildest dreams to the moment I open my eyes to wake, the thought of you always drives me crazy. I can't seem to get enough of you.

>I can see you...
>I can hear you...
>I can feel you...
>I can smell you...
>I can sense you...

I can't walk by you without even greeting you with an official hello and a smile! You're just too good to pass up. I can't ever ignore you as if you're some stranger on the street. Your light shines so bright... you bring life into every room. Your anointing fills every space... even the space inside my heart and the sacred space at the altar! I notice the way you interact with other people; you treat them like pure gold. When I observe you, I think of you as a diamond that is one in a million. The closer I get to you, I can feel the heat between us. I can never pass up the chance to give you a warm embrace.

Your beautiful face brings joy to my soul. Your radiant smile sparkles like expensive pearls. Whenever you speak, I hang on to every word. It's sweet like honey that I imagine dripping from those insatiable lips. It would be my pleasure to taste them one day. I'm in such awe of you... I tremble with passion whenever you're near me. You really give me butterflies inside. You're too good to pass up because I never want to let go of your hand. Your energy is too good to pass up because I enjoy absorbing it. Your faithfulness is too good to pass up because I admire the godly woman that you are. I would be blind or very stupid to pass someone like you up! Not trying to sound needy or desperate... it just feels so good to be around you! The treasure inside of you is too good to pass up! The blessing that is on you is too good to pass up! The thought of making you my future wife is too good to pass up!

I'm so glad you pulled up on my life the way you did. I was lost in the fog, but you shined through and gave me hope once again! I thank God for you! It's really an honor to know you. My eyes water with tender affection and admiration for you. If you were a ship, I would welcome the opportunity to come on board because you're too good to pass up! Together we could sail away to our favorite destination... love, a place too good to pass up.

# ECHO OF LOVE

## By Aaron Woodson

My love echoes out to the world like dolphins using echolocation. I'm sending out these good vibrations. What's being transmitted or communicated doesn't seem to be so loud and clear. It's strange being in the unfamiliar territory of loneliness. Gotta keep on swimming or else I'll drown in a sea of depression. Excuse my expression, but I've been searching for this treasure of love like a pirate. I just want to seize the moment and make that special someone all mine. However, I'm waiting on the LORD to bring her to me. He knows my heart's intentions. He knows me inside and out without a doubt. His love keeps me alive and is the greatest of all. Now I can truly show the world of what I'm made of... LOVE.

# SHOTS FIRED

## By Aaron Woodson

What I thought was love has now left me riddled with shots and given me these puncturing wounds. She emptied out the whole clip on me. But if I'm really honest, I took my shots and fired back with relentless assault. We are both bleeding out pain and misery. We were both at fault in this tragic incident. Now I'm seeing flashbacks before all this happened... we were once a happy and beautiful couple. We used to have each other's back. Yeah, we used to go toe to toe, but we always found a way to kiss and make up. We were loyal to each other. We were black royalty. You were my queen who always knew how to wear her crown. I was your robe, and together we were wrapped in greatness, power, and luxury. You were always glorious in my eyes. I was simply marvelous in your eyes too. There was no other love that could rival the kind of love we shared. I never thought we would become casualties in love that became war. Love can't ever be defeated, but it surely knows how to be submissive. Rebellion on the other hand is dismissive. Our behavior escalated from passive to aggressive suddenly... guess we ignored the signs. Hearts weren't ever designed to take all this abuse. Being angry, hurt, or offended is no excuse for any of this. We both need to take some responsibility. We need some accountability. I was hoping we could somehow find stability. We have the ability to forgive one another and move forward, yet we're both too stubborn to say we are sorry. We just kill ourselves by being stupid. We need to stop pulling the trigger... we both know what happens when we do. The only trigger I wish for you to pull is the one that I pack. I'm always loaded, but somehow you'll make me go empty. I need to reload, but it's too late... you already got me.

# ERUPTION

## By Aaron Woodson

Dating in these millennial times is so delusional. The rules have changed, and the game is played much differently nowadays. Attraction is a vibe that has been killed so much that it's becoming extinct. Feelings are trapped inside looking for a way out, yet they remain incarcerated. Freedom of expression is no longer encouraged. People are so sensitive now! Labels are so quick to get tossed at you. Too much judgment and not enough empathy... but for real, I don't need your sympathy. I need you to stop justifying your weird behavior. You always want to be right... sometimes you just need to get checked like a pair of Nikes. Now let me go ahead and testify. You treated me like I was a fly on the wall. You tried to swat me away, but I remained loyal and kept coming back to you. Eventually, though, I had enough, and I had to fly away. You always went for those sly guys instead of me. It's all good. I'm still a fly guy, and like Jim Jones, I still FLY HIGH and you know I'm ballin'! You know I just did my own thing... you heard I became successful and wanted to be a part of my life. This ship has sailed, and now you can go kick rocks. But there are no hard feelings... no animosity or love lost. Sometimes you have to go away for a while and then come back. You wanted the bad boys for as long as I've known you... now you're with the one you really want. Funny how things work out, right? I'm still winning and grinning without you anywhere near me! I'll get a real one, and together we'll make a dream team. I'm just glad to move on and forget about this nightmare. The future is brighter now that I see the bigger picture!

# RADAR

## By Aaron Woodson

I'm picking up something... I wonder what it could be.
From my view, it's not what I see but more like, Who is that? She is unlike anyone I've ever seen before. There must be a reason that she came up on my radar! Words can't do her any justice... I'd give her plenty of heart emoji's, though! She got me locked in. I am making my approach like a stealth torpedo. I need my delivery to land like a heat-seeking missile! I've got nothing to lose, and neither does she. Maybe we'll make some fireworks, who knows? Our eyes make contact, we are now engaged onto one another. I work my charm like magic, she appears like she can't resist... or can she? I got to play my cards right so I can get the upper hand. I'm working with a full deck. She definitely is working with something too! Her sexy, warm, and inviting smile makes the chocolate melt off of my body. I can tell my cool and calm demeanor is driving her wild! My pheromones are permeating throughout the air, so she catches a good whiff of my cologne. She gets turned on by the fragrance and asks me what I'm wearing. I smile and confidently say, "Blue Chanel."

She replies, "You smell really good." I know I got this one in the bag. I tell her I'd like to take her out sometime, and I ask for her phone number. The moment of truth... drum roll is going on in my head. Survey says... To my surprise she gives me her number and tells me to call her. My swagger was strong tonight. I smile again and let her know it was a pleasure. I'll definitely keep in touch. I had to be on her radar too... It's not every day you find a guy like me. It's a win-win for both of us. Use your radar for potential prospects... you'll pick up the right one!

# PERSPECTIVES OF LOVE

By Karli LeMay & Aaron Woodson

You say you love me,
Only the best intentions.
You want me to have the best,
So baby, let me. (Karli L.)

I loved you with every fiber of my soul.
I thought I knew your worth, guess I came up a little short. (Aaron W.)

You say you'd never hurt me,
But when we talk it's like a game...
Of how can you manipulate
So that things remain the same. (Karli L.)

I know I wasn't perfect, but neither were you.
I believed we could become whole despite our imperfections.
We reflected good and bad tendencies like a
mirror, we saw right through each other. (Aaron W.)

You praise God for a woman like me,
But when did He say
That is how it should be?
Want me to feel His peace,
So baby, let me. (Karli L.)

Yes, I sure did sing your praises.
I thought you were heaven sent, at
least, that's how I pictured it. Things changed.

You talk about feeling His peace... but I was left
with you disturbing my peace. Constant nagging
like a broken record! That's the way I remember it
being framed in my mind. (Aaron W.)

Suppressing my emotions,
Fear of how you may react.
"How will he handle the truth?"
Can I just go back...
To when I just felt free,
To when I felt like me. (Karli L.)

You make it sound like you were caged up in a prison
this whole time! I'm not your prison warden, I never kept
you on lockdown. I feel like I'm the one standing trial and
waiting to hear my sentence. Guess the "truth" shall set us
free! (Aaron W.)

Before I got lost in these feelings,
That would never be...
True to myself.
True to what I want.
In hopes you may be the one,
That I almost forgot... (Karli L.)

While you got lost in your feelings,
I was left confused, trying to read your mind!
It was too little, too late to find out that you
were more comfortable with yourself than you
ever were with me! (Aaron W.)

Without you, I am whole

By the Lover of my soul,
With the One who's my supplier,
And knows my heart's desire.
Want me to feel His perfect love,
So baby, let me. (Karli L.)

Baby, I understand...
So I will give you what your heart desires,
Only because I know that is what He requires for us
to be whole again! (Aaron W.)

Telling you what you want to hear,
I even believe it too.
Beautiful words that sound complete
While inside I'm torn in two. (Karli L.)

It shouldn't have been this way...
Or should it? We were too busy trying to write
our own love story when it was God writing it this whole
entire time. We kept on trying to steal the pen! (Aaron W.)

Why does it have to be so hard?
God, I just want to know what's right.
Not realizing that all along,
I put myself in this fight. So no longer will I let you
hold me back from being me. No longer will I let you
convince me that being free involves the idea of me and
you, 'cause now I know what is to be true. That I don't owe
you these pieces of my heart, so I'm taking them back for
good. You could never give me what I need,
How did you think you could?
So, baby, let me,

Let me... go (Karli L.)

I never wanted to let you go, but go and be free! We were on borrowed time anyway; eventually I feared that this would happen. I have peace in my heart that I did the very best I could for you. I'm sorry that wasn't enough for you. There's always a villain in every story and apparently it was me. Too bad I wasn't the hero you were looking for. I couldn't save us this time. So I won't clip your wings because in my eyes you'll always be an angel of mine.
So fly away my love,
Just let me...
just let me be (Aaron W.)

# WHAT IS LOVE?

## By Aaron Woodson

Been stabbed by the knife of betrayal, I'm seriously wounded. I'm in desperate need of some miraculous healing. I'm bleeding from my soul... I didn't want to cry foul, but what I'm experiencing is way beyond that! Even an umpire can see that from a mile away. It seems like I've struck out so many times when stepping up to the plate. Yo, why she dog me out like that? Why am I all alone in the dugout? I thought we made it all the way home, but someone else stole my base. Was I out of position? I thought I played it safe... but maybe that wasn't such a good idea. After all, we are meant to take some risks from time to time. I thought I was winning, but all this time I was losing. Love should have prevailed, right? Did I have the heart to love you the way that I should? You know I woulda. Or I shoulda. Or coulda... so obviously I missed something. No one deserves to be hurt. However, pain is all part of the process in growth. Forgiveness is for you, not them! You have to set yourself free and embrace love once more... cowards hide, but real men face what's in front of them! It's OK to fall, but don't stay down. Get back up and keep fighting. Love is worth fighting for. God is love, and He fought for our love on the cross. We were worth it to Him. He is the perfect example of what love looks like! I try to comprehend love, but it goes deeper than my understanding is capable of. I'm learning and I'm healing because I know Jesus loves me. He's all I'll ever want and need.

# YOU'RE MY FIRST LOVE

By Aaron Woodson

You were the first love I've ever known. The first thought I have is of me waking up to your lovely face. When I gaze into your eyes, I know that I can face tomorrow. I see forever with you; we have grown so attached to one another like Legos! We are building for the future; I am sure what we make will be built to last. Whatever happened in our past is not welcome in our present. We are God's special gift to one another. We wrap each other with the finest love. We fit together like a hand that meets a glove. When push comes to shove, I know we have each other's back. If I'm on my back, I know you're there to lift me up. I wouldn't let you be on your back when I can put you on my back. We can get through anything, baby, just you and me. We can ascend to greatness as long as we learn the true meaning of meekness. You're my weakness. Let us look to God because, in our weakness, His strength is more than sufficient. Without Him we would be nothing. Let me rephrase this statement. I used to think of you as my first love, but that isn't completely true. You're the love of my life, but God will always and forever be my first love!

# LOVE STILL MATTERS

By Aaron Woodson

Most people nowadays are getting a divorce. They decide to change course and show no remorse, would rather split than keep it together. Birds of a feather flock together, but y'all wanna rock the boat and let it sink instead of trying to keep it afloat! Not judging you, that's your business... just saying it's not a good look. It's bad for the culture. People became entitled to what's theirs; they forgot what it was like to share. Now they don't even care. Divorces have now become a scavenger hunt. Somebody always takes more than they should, like vultures swoopin' in to devour every last morsel of the carcass. They leave the other person with next to nothing. It's almost like they have been stripped naked. Court battles over assets, but you surrendered your marriage and didn't even want to fight for it. Took the easy way out... you can give all the excuses you want to, I ain't buyin' it! Some people should never get married. They do it for the wrong reasons. Some people are "goal-diggers," not just gold-diggers. Did you catch that? Others are opportunists, manipulators, and control freaks! Don't worry, I'm about to put this all to bed. Everyone makes their own bed, so they have no choice but to sleep in it. It's time to stop seeing marriage as a curse or punishment and start seeing it as a true blessing. I know it's not easy to stay in love... but I don't understand why you would throw it all away in the trash? I get it, sometimes people clash, but don't you think divorce is a little rash? When that happens we need to make a mad dash to the altar and pray, the same altar where we exchanged our vows and said, "I do!" We have our differences, but we need to discover our common ground. Divorce and breaking up families is absurd and ridiculous! I'm no expert on the matter, but that's just my take on it. Love still matters!

# DANCING PARTNERS

By Amaryllis Del Moral Rivera (Amaryllis) & Aaron Woodson

Dancing to me is much more than just "dancing." Dance begins with the kind of song I enjoy. It is also more to be desired than just the lyrics of a song. Yes, there might be some good songs out there with a nice beat to the lyrics. There are also some "not so great" lyrics with a catchy beat that can almost fool anyone into believing it's even a good song. And then of course there's always the song where either the beat or the lyrics are straight trash.

You see, I understand music, not just lyrics or the computerized sounds and rhythms that are very popular these days. I studied music during my high school years and was part of a chorus. That being said, my relationship is with music itself, partner or not! Dancing showed up in my life later, and the rest is history.

I aspired to be a dancer in the past, but it didn't happen for me. Military life and Zumba are responsible for that relationship I now enjoy with dance. When Zumba was created, for me it just made perfect sense. A format that allowed me to be a dancer... it knew exactly the type of music I wanted to dance with. And as an added bonus, dance helped me get in shape, energized me, and gave me an overall confidence boost.

Today, not only do I dance for myself, but I look for better ways of improving the transmission of knowledge and understanding of movement in relationship with music for others. Although the older gym industry didn't really focus on developing a good musical ear or on working the body in a balanced way, it did bring excitement and fun to the atmosphere. I absolutely love this music, dance, and fitness relationship that Zumba brought into my life. I believe that it is a gateway to influence many people to live an overall healthier and happier lifestyle!

(Aaron)
Music is my obsession. It puts me in such a hypnotic trance. My body voluntarily moves to the music. This is where my dancing begins to take over! My body speaks a rhythm only few can understand. My steps are fluid and are like divinity in motion. I love to dip, slip, glide, slide, step, jerk, and pop-lock. Nothing about my dance routine is choreographed... I'm all freestyle, baby!

When I'm dancing it's like I'm married to the song that is playing in that very moment. Music grabs my attention. It captivates and mesmerizes me. When I look across the dance floor, I find a dance partner to keep up with my pace. Only space separates us, but soon we shall close the distance.

I've always been the kind of guy to dance to the beat of my own drum. Now it looks like that has changed since this encounter. Something about you keeps me engaged. There is definitely something special about you and the way you move!

Together, we know how to groove. I study you like I'm preparing for an exam. You teach me so much about grace, and I teach you about style. There is an art to dancing. It's excitement waiting to happen and memories just waiting to be made.

You, my sweet lady, have made a lasting impression on me. I believe I've done the same for you. Music plus dancing equals attraction! The smiles we exchange are quite pleasant. Music brought us here.

We were meant to meet each other. We weren't looking for anything serious... it just so happened that we were curious! Neither of us could recall any previous encounters we've had before. Somehow this feels all too familiar, yet refreshing at the same time.

Eventually the music stops. Now we have a dilemma. Do we continue this someplace else, or do we go our separate ways? Hmmm. One lesson I've learned from dancing is that you must show up! I hope that when I show up to this place again you will meet me here once more. It's not every day an opportunity like this comes along. I don't need you, but I want you. I want you to be my dancing partner for life!

# PATTERNS OF SEXY

By Aaron Woodson

What does sexy mean to you? There are many ways to define sexy. People have their own versions or interpretations of sex appeal! For me, "sexy" is an artistic expression! It can also be associated with having an exhilarating facial expression. Sexy is a noun or verb depending on who you ask! Sexy has always existed, way before time.

Sexy is a brand you advertise. Be advised, sexy is a product that sells! As you can probably tell, I enjoy sexy a lot. I wake up next to her, and she makes me feel some type of way. I even lie down with sexy in my dreams! Finding your identity is sexy because you find out why you were created to be what you're becoming! Sexy is the cream on top; it's a flavor that never loses its taste. Sexy can never be stale; everything else just pales in comparison to it!

Wine, candles, and flowers to go with a nice meal are sexy. Being nude isn't the only thing that is sexy! Sexy is never rude or pushy. It is a polite visitor that wants to be welcomed to satisfy you! Sexy exudes confidence and knows how to get attention. Sexy definitely has my attention. Every now and then I give her a win, make her think about the good times we've had.

Sexy can be very subtle. Sexy can be very inviting and quite a warm welcome. She knows exactly what she be doing too! Sexy knows how to walk that walk and talk that talk. Sexy speaks my favorite languages, all six romantic love languages wrapped in one, plus body language. Sexy comes and goes as she pleases. Sexy turns me on! I can't get enough of sexy. Truth is I can never outgrow sexy. Sexy is in my DNA! Sexy is very desirable and quite suitable for me! Sexy comes in many shades, colors, shapes, and forms... together it's the total package!

I believe sexy was an invention. No one should ever feel guilty for feeling sexy. Sexy is comforting when it needs to be. Sexy needs to be safe. Y'all know what I'm talking about. Sexy has a right to be exercised and it's fit for everyone! If sexy were a fabric, it sure would look amazing for you to wear! Sexy is worn in all four seasons... Spring, summer, winter, and fall! Sexy is always in style and in perfect fashion!

Sexy can adapt to anything. It's our companion or reassurance. Being godly is sexy! There is just something about that anointing that just gets to my spirit! There ain't no crime in being sexy or feeling sexy! Ain't no shame in being or feeling sexy. Let sexy do her thing... she makes such beautiful patterns! Patterns are made to follow. The patterns of sexy have been designed for us to share with each other. Let's enjoy them while we still can... get your sexy on!

# BY FAITH

By Aaron Woodson

I feel a vibe—it's contagious. Look into your eyes, it's dangerous. Steppin' outside my comfort zone is courageous. Baby, we ain't meant to be no strangers. I'm on the front lines—you could easily shoot me down!—yet here we are standing face to face. One of us has to pull the trigger. I think it's gonna be me. I'm well equipped for this kind of situation. This isn't no infatuation... this is a real genuine interest I have in you. Before you think of saying no, just think of why you should say YES! I'm in position. I've put myself all the way out here to get close to you. I am drawn to you. I am drawn to you. Even if I tried to pull away, like Tyrese, something just keeps pulling me back, telling me I need you in my life. I need you to hear me, OK? God made no mistakes. He brought us together at this moment in time. I need you to know that I want to go out with you sometime. Tell me what you think about that? You're looking at me quizzically and analyzing my body language. I think you're fluent in what I'm speaking to you right now. I know you understand what I'm telling you. We grown, we ain't kids no more! This ain't no playground, but believe me, I know how to play when it comes to that. This isn't a game, but at the same time it kinda is. Will this be a game of chess or poker? We both can win if you choose the right answer. But whatever the outcome, I accept it. You look at me and start to move those succulent lips. You're looking at me like I'm some kind of a snack. Baby, I don't mind being your appetizer! Your posture is stationary but calm. Words slowly begin to echo the answer I've been waiting for. Oh, the anticipation! You resoundingly said, much to my surprise, "Yes, you sure can!" That's all I needed, baby! Thank you, Jesus, Hallelujah! I had my conviction; you gave me my affirmation, but God gave me confirmation it was all in His miraculous timing. Praise

His name! He is so good! I've been praying for someone like you for a mighty long time. I was a brother in waiting, but now I'm a man that is blessed and highly favored! By faith, you made all this possible. LORD, thank you!
Thank you! Thank you! I'm sleeping good tonight. I mean that truly because it was all by faith!

# YOU JUST GOT SERVED

By Aaron Woodson

Poetry is something I've always cooked up. My words are marinated with my own personal seasonings. I'm the chef that serves you something nice and hot on the platter. Nutrition matters! My poetry is gourmet; I come with the sauce! I'll be your alfredo or marinara; I'm not your average meatball. My baby wants all my pasta. She can't seem to get enough. Trust, I know how to prepare a good and nutritious meal of carbs. I'm her favorite aroma. She can't help but follow her nose. She might be nosey or maybe just a bit more curious. My recipe for love will have her wanting more and more. Her desire alone is not enough to quench her thirst for me. I'm like fine wine: she can't help but enjoy my quality of taste. Neither of us can afford to let all this go to waste. I'm her dinner tonight! There won't be any leftovers. My poetry contains insatiable flavor that has all the preservatives needed to make this love last forever! Don't forget how you just got served!

# IT'S A DONE DEAL

## By Aaron Woodson

Your smile is bona fide gorgeous. I can't stress enough how captivating it truly is. You disarm me with your sweet and contagious demeanor! I think you got me falling in love. Wait a minute, is that considered a felony or misdemeanor? If I committed any kind of offense, please go ahead and arrest me now! I want to stand trial and surrender these rights of mine over to you! I want you to sentence me. I'm guilty until proven innocent. Lock me up and throw away the key! No telling what would happen between us behind closed doors. I'm so deep in my feelings; you got me feeling some type of way! Anxiety is reaching the ceiling. This attraction is killing me. I want to be your man but at the same time be your lawyer. I want to make sure you're well represented as my client. We are building a case for intimacy! My fervent desire has reached the exceeding Fahrenhiet. I know you feel the scorching passion between me and you. The chemistry is hot like lava. We could melt down these walls that surround us with all this volcanic activity going on up in here. We definitely want each other's smoke. I imagine myself sitting at your table and sipping on a glass of moscato. I want to taste your essence and feel your gifted touch. Am I doing too much? Let me know if I need to fall back and let you take control. Put me under your spell. I can see you're really enjoying this, but now watch how tables can easily turn. Now I got you right where I want you, all in these arms of mine because I can't see me ever letting go. We're made for each other. We're a perfect fit—or should I say pair! I think it's fair enough to assume we are official now! I think we can put a ring on it. Are you down? OK, cool. You can even add my last name to it! It's a done deal!

# I KNOW MY WORTH

## By Aaron Woodson

You see me for these dollar signs... I come with the proverbial price tag! I stay getting my bag, yet every time I get a little something you got your hands all out. You always show me your hands. Why don't you show me your heart? I guess the prerequisite for dating someone like you is a cash advance or some kind of collateral.

I wish our values ran parallel, but they are much different like the many kinds of designer apparel you see in department stores. You got quite a shoe fetish, you have quite the embellished collection, but why can't you ever be content with just one selection? You're so indecisive about the size you wear. I got the pair that fits you just perfectly.

I know you want to look all glamorous and all that, but I got that good comfort for you and I'll even lace you up with my one of a kind style. I know I'm not everyone's cup of tea. I would enjoy it very much if you at least took one sip of me! I don't come lukewarm. I come fresh and hot. But somehow I'm invisible when I don't have what you want or require me to have.

Money is your motto. They say cash is king, but all I ever wanted was to give you a ring. Baby, I'll always sing your praises, you been heard my beat! You know my song, and you damn sure know its fire! I been turned up the heat... now you sweatin' me for more shit to give you. All you want to do is take. Man, how much more can I take? For goodness' sake, give my wallet a break!

I can't deal with your sense of entitlement. I'm a legitimate hustler. I don't mind breaking bread, but I'm starting to get the feeling you're using and abusing me like a substance. You get high off of what I provide for you, kind of like the relationship between an addict and a drug dealer! You like what I sell, but you never wanna buy! Maybe you just need the right fix. It's time you found a new supplier. I'm taking my business elsewhere. I'm setting up shop for my bride-to-be. Until then I'm just gonna chill and hold it down. I know my worth.

# SHOULD HAVE BEEN MORE CAREFUL
By Aaron Woodson

You wear bitterness as the latest fashion; I thought hate went out of style. I guess it never went anywhere and decided to stay. As I lie in my bed, I can't help but think of the great memories we once shared. Everything came to a screeching halt, then came the verbal assaults. Feels like my mind had been doing somersaults; been chastised for all my faults, yet you can't seem to see past yours. I can admit when I'm wrong. With you, it's the same old sad song. How long are you going to keep singing the blues? My heart is like fragile guitar strings: you just about broke every last one of them. No wonder I'm out of tune. People are like delicate instruments: we need to learn how to understand their rhythm. We have to feel their vibrations. I only wanted to match your circadian rhythm or even just be in sync with your heartbeat. Our behavioral patterns toward each other have become irregular. There is no harmony within each other's company any longer. We haven't been on the same page for quite some time. Statistics show that divorce has been on a rampage for years. It's a cancer, something I am desperately trying to avoid. I'm paranoid that this most likely will happen to us. I don't want this, but if it comes down to it then so be it! Hate and bitterness come with consequences. We should have been more careful!

# SUNFLOWER

By Aaron Woodson

Throughout my life and just about everywhere I've gone, I've tried to plant seeds. This world is full of beautiful vegetation, and among the population, you and only you caught my gaze. When I look at you, I'm in a daze. Damn, this is crazy! Thank you for being a flower among the weeds... I'm so glad you weren't born with thorns! It seems as if you were meant to be planted in my life. I promise to take good care of you. My nose was open to your inviting, sweet scent. I breathe in your essence. Oh, I just love being in your presence. You and me make perfect sense. Our time together is certainly well spent! I will make sure I shower you daily with pure love. The sun gives you the spotlight you deserve. You brighten up each day for me! Thank you for being my lovely and wonderful sunflower!

# INTRIGUING LOVE

By Aaron Woodson

Lately, I've noticed how passive-aggressive you've become toward me. I've also noticed how sarcastic I've been. Our behavior toward each other is unnecessary, and it doesn't tell the whole story. I'm not trying to make it about whose right or wrong; it's about getting closer to resolving our conflict. Neither of us are perfect, but we are most certainly perfect together! We both have our expectations. Maybe we can put those aside and focus on having a good conversation. I feel like I'm always in good company with you despite our differences! You fascinate me. I always wonder what's going on with that beautiful mind of yours. I know the things I do have; you're curious and wondering about me sometimes too! I can't figure you out. You can't figure me out! We are both unpredictable; now it's time for us to be inseparable. The night belongs to us. Let's make it right under the beautiful, star-studded night sky. When I look into your precious eyes, I see a doorway into a breathtaking dimension. I'm drawn to you, and I just want to enter your sacred temple. Let's keep this simple: I want to hear the melodies of affection echoing from your passionate lips. I could write a book on how you're making me feel right now. I have such an appetite for you. I want you for breakfast, lunch, and dinner. My palate can never get enough of you; that's why I always want you for my dessert. I'm asserting myself as a man and inserting you into this plan, but ultimately, we are part of God's plan! Will you come into agreement and alignment with me in the presence of God to make a covenant? I have a calling on my life. You have a calling on your life. Our worlds have collided for a reason. In this season, I want to make you my wife. I hope you would like me to be your husband. I don't want to force your hand, only to ask for it so I could put this ring on it. Mrs. Woodson has a nice ring to it, doesn't it? Destiny awaits us. The past is behind us now. The present is here, and our future awaits us. Let us walk together in peace, harmony, and love! I'll meet you at the altar... I'll see you soon, baby—save the date! Let's make it official and get that notarized! I can't help that this love just hypnotizes me! Your love intrigues me. That should excite you... now let that entice you.

# LOVE SONG

## By Aaron Woodson

I write the lyrics, and you're the melody to this beautiful song called love. We make the perfect duet. This collaboration between us is like no other. I enjoy hearing the beautiful notes we sing together. We are each other's favorite instrument; we always know how to get the best out of one another. We've been through many stages. When we decided to bring out love on tour, we didn't know what all this would lead to. We felt it was only right to be a couple. Some people out there thought that we were crazy to be in love. We had a vision of love, and it has manifested into something special that neither of us could have ever imagined! It hasn't always been all roses; sometimes you have to deal with the thorns. Remember that Jesus has a crown of them on His head too. In this life, pain comes with pleasure. Sometimes things go wrong; just learn to play along. You will fall flat at times and simply be off-key. That's OK, just remember to find your rhythm. Love is the driving force behind this harmonious arrangement. We kiss our fears goodbye, wipe each other's tears, and put on our best show! We sing and play our hearts out for each other. Nothing ever can quite compare to this! Our love song is a chart topper. In our eyes we are number one, and we will stay there for as long as possible!

# RING MY BELL/SOUND THE ALARM

By Aaron Woodson

I hear bells and whistles going off around me! There is an indication that triggers into my brain that something just might be wrong. Or it could be something that is trying to get my attention. I don't want to be caught unaware, so I respond to the disturbance. I'm trying to figure out what's setting these alarms off. Maybe there is a party going on inside of my head. Hopefully, I'm not just hearing things. Maybe there is a sound that only I can hear. I feel like bells and alarms give people a sense of urgency to what is happening or what needs to happen in that moment! Sometimes it may be God's way of getting your attention. The world can keep us distracted, and we can miss or overlook certain details in life. When something doesn't look right or seem right, it would be wise to sound the alarm. Alarms are a sign of distress, caution, or to be observant. New cars usually have all the bells, whistles, and sirens. Most people like to purchase these vehicles with all the latest and greatest features. Therefore, we tend to become creatures of habit! There are alarms that I purposely love to activate. I'm talking about the alarms on my lady's fine body. I know exactly what sets her off. I can silence her if need be, but I just enjoy the sweet sounds that echo on our bedroom walls! I have alarms too. Only she knows how to ring my bell and sound my alarm!

# SUMMER DRESSES

By Aaron Woodson

Every season there is a variety of fashionable trends that are in style. There is a certain attire that gets my attention and just never seems to fade away. I'm so blown away by what it brings in. I'm starting to get tunnel vision; everything else around me is getting blurry. All I see is beautiful, exotic, and sexy women wearing summer dresses! Goodness, gracious! Lord, have mercy... Summer dresses are a blessing. Can I get a amen? I'm so thankful that summer dresses were made. You can see them being worn in the sun or shade. As many as I see on the daily, I swear I was surrounded by a parade of summer dresses. They come in all different, colors, shapes, patterns, and designs. Summer dresses are quite divine. They breathe easy, but they certainly can make any man speechless. Summer dresses are so form-fitting... I just love how they hug certain physiques. Ladies that wear them have many diverse techniques on how they want to show theirs off. There is a bold and elevated confidence from these gorgeous specimens walking around God's green earth! Like Chingy, I like the way they do that "right thurr!" Most men can't help but stare. Can you blame them, though? Ladies, you know what you be doing with them summer dresses on! That's definitely the easiest way to turn me on, just sayin'! My temperature goes all the way up... no wonder I'm gettin' all feverish! I see the look in their eyes, seems so devilish! They may not wanna tempt me 'cause I'm about ready to unleash the beast on 'em! It doesn't take much for a brother like me to get aroused. Hips don't lie and neither do those eyes. Summer dresses are just so hypnotic. They make me turn into such a romantic. I enjoy the round of applause I get. It's pretty erotic! Quite ironic, isn't it? The way y'all prance around in them Summer Dressed just make me want to get up and dance! I heard about them freak-'em dresses, but summer dresses have to be the next best thing! You can spot them almost any time and anywhere. Winter time, probably not so much. Summer dresses can make any man thirsty! I know I have a free show, so I got me a glass to sip on already. I'm thinkin' any of these women would be down for a little bubbly. I would give a toast to any summer dress I see on deck! Summer dresses are a dream come true. I'm putting a BOLO out on these summer dresses. They are WANTED! No crimes have been committed yet. The scene is safe. Not a hater or jacker in sight. Like Cube, I say today was a good day! For all the women in the place with style and grace, we say thank you and God bless you for wearing those sexy summer dresses! Hope to see you wearing them next summer.

# DOWNLOADED

### By Aaron Woodson

If you were a program, I'd download you into my life. Our sweet conversation is buffering and loading into this wonderful and mesmerizing program called attraction. Your HDMI is connected to my chassis. You're like a router, and I'm the switch on the motherboard: together we make a great connection. We can't just settle for any old affection. Let's put in a boot sequence, explore some of our favorite settings. What's on the menu? Let's input a command and configure our systems. I got all the right connections; I just need to insert my device. Does that fit OK? Isn't that nice? I get in where I plug in. We charge up each other's power supply; love is definitely circulating all over us now. Time to upload sweet memory lane and activate this passion. I got plenty of sticks of RAM. Baby, just give me ROM so I can read your thoughts and feelings. I want us to stay on the same network forever. Communication is a must, and trust that ain't no lie. No need for us to keep secret passwords from each other; we are encrypted. One last thing, I'm sending you a kiss, and I hope you store all of me on your internal heart drive always. And the same goes for me with you. Together, in this life and the next, we are fully downloaded for one another. COMPUTER LOVE is now complete.

# TRAMPOLINE

## By Aaron Woodson

Before there were bouncing kids' playhouses, there were trampolines. It was always fun to jump around and go as high as you could to touch the sky. Trampolines were innovative and enjoyable for their time. They still find them to be the life of the party. Kids of all ages can be seen jumping all over the place. Bouncing on a rubber canvas supported by spring tension seems pretty repetitive, but I know when I was bouncing on the trampoline, I never wanted to stop. It felt good to get high as I could in the air. It was a great workout for sure. Speaking of workouts, when me and my sweet lover meet up in person, we find ourselves on a king-size mattress. It's a place we really enjoy spending our time together. The bed we perform our acrobatic stunts on is like our trampoline. There is a whole lot of bouncing in between the sheets. I'm always concerned about the weight capacity of a bed's support but also the trampoline's. I can bet a few trampolines have been broken due to overuse and overweight limits. I've broken in some beds before, but I've never actually broken a bed during intercourse. Now if that were to happen, I would laugh hysterically but would take the action to the floor. Shit, I'll be the trampoline. My honey bounce on me like a low rider on hydraulics. There would be no resistance from me whatsoever. I can't even see myself on a trampoline now; the way my weight is set up I might just break it! I know I'd break the bottom out. The force is with me. I can see Yoda telling me, "Very heavy and strong you are!" I can hear my lady sayin', "Go ahead, Daddy... You can always be my trampoline!"

# IT'S TIME THAT WE SPEAK

By Aaron Woodson

I want to talk, but at this moment we are only talking in silence. It just doesn't make any sense. Sometimes I'm on the fence. Don't know if I should reach out or if I should allow you to make that move. My words aren't always heard, so when I'm quiet, just know and understand that my silence speaks volumes!

We used to be able to feel one another's flames. We would always welcome each other with warm exchanges. However, something has noticeably changed. Maybe one of us changed or perhaps both. It's hard to speculate and articulate the pain that is being experienced between us right now. One day, I thought I heard a knock at my door and assumed it was you, but it was just my imagination. I seem to have this stranger in my house known as separation, and somehow it's made itself welcome in my presence.

I always had this fascination with you. You were my favorite sensation and even sometimes my sweetest temptation. We've been through so many valleys and rivers together. Like Marvin, I believe there is no mountain high enough to keep my love from getting to you. I need you and I want you, right here, right now. Foolish pride shouldn't hold my feelings captive inside. My soul is pouring out through my eyes.

I thank God for you. My love for you is deeper than any reservoir. You're a reflection of what I always dreamed, and you will always be transcribed on the memoir of my heart! You're the song I always think of singing when I wake up in the morning. I praise God for you! I got those happy feet, and you just make me want to get up and dance! Baby, let's give this another chance.

Let's make it last forever! Where I go, you go. Where you go, I go! Let's keep it on a high note. You're my soprano, and I'll always be your tender, loving tenor! You're more than my muse. You're the fire to my fuse. I refuse to let this fire go out. You're the fire, and I'm the desire. We are all we need. That's all that should be required! No more breaks. Now it's time that we finally speak!

# MISSED OPPORTUNITY

By Aaron Woodson

I always thought you would think of me as your man crush. I tried to say clever things just to make you blush, but you weren't feelin' me that way. I was fascinated by you, so it would only make sense to be fastened to you. The attraction made me feel some type of way. I was blown away. I was the fly on the wall trying to create some kind of buzz. I wasn't even on your radar... maybe I sent the wrong signal. I wanted to be your hero and make your day, but I guess I'm the creep who's the villain. You're like Harley Quinn, you love being with those jokers! You give me the poker face, or should I say the resting bitch face. Not really a surprise there. I wanted to give you a sneak preview of what a real man is like, but you ain't ready. I know I should have no expectations, but my preparation to even speak to you and show confidence should give me some brownie points at least! The only thing I can think of is that I'm overqualified to fill the position to satisfy you. My resume speaks volumes. Maybe you should carefully reconsider. But it's OK, everyone makes choices. I guess it just wasn't meant to be. Live and learn, crash and burn, only to live with regret. I'm up right now, so down the road when you think back, don't forget to thank me for giving you the time of day. By the time you realize it, I'll be too busy living the good life... so sorry you missed out!

# LADIES ONLY

By Aaron Woodson

Some ladies just don't get it. You look at most men as only "providers" and not much else. Maybe you find amusement with us being toys you want to play with. In all honesty, hearts are not meant to be played with at all. But it's like you don't even care or even comprehend your behavior. You're always so quick to point the finger at us about our behavior, yet you don't seem to play by the same rules. Where is the accountability? Men offer so much more than you realize, but you seem a little confused. You don't seem to know what you really want. So tell me what you want, I mean what you really, really want. You don't want my time. You don't want the truth. You don't want to give me what I deserve. You don't want to trust me. You don't want to listen to me. You don't even want any of my love. I just think you're all in it for yourself. It's all about you. The only thing you seem to want from us men is money, material things, and dick. You don't really value a man like he should be treated. He should be treated like a king! There are plenty of guys I know who would give up everything for the woman they love. Would you even do the same? Sounds a little one-sided to me. I don't mean to sound pessimistic, but this is the reality that we are facing today as men. Do we matter? You matter to us... at least the majority of us! I can't speak for everyone, but you know what I'm sayin'. Where is the love? Where is the respect? Where is the honor? This poem isn't a complaint; this is a plea to all women. Be good to your man. Love your man. Respect your man. Honor your man. Trust your man. Defend your man! Help your man! Pray for your man! Stand by your man! Don't leave when shit gets hard. You wanna soldier, but you won't even stand and fight when it matters most. I thought you were a ride-or-die chick, but now you wanna run off and hide. It was so convenient for you to leave, wasn't it? But that's OK, I'll be all right! Just go and leave us with the short end of the stick. Don't worry, this guy will come out on top again! In fact, all of us guys will for that matter. If you wanna lay with dogs, then just know you'll catch some fleas. Men don't own you, ladies, you're free to do whatever you desire. But understand, there are rewards and consequences for your actions. Real talk! This one is for the ladies.

# NEW NARRATIVE

By Aaron Woodson

You see me coming, but you find every possible way to avoid me. I'm not coming for you; you just so happen to be in my path. I'm no threat to you and you're no threat to me. I don't have beef unless you're just being chicken. When I see your face you look like you're sucking on a lemon. Are you really that sour? Can you even stand the sight of my light? There is no need to retreat into your little shell of darkness. I don't believe it's really you that has a problem with me. It's what people have been whispering in your ear about me. It's also the principalities at work within you. I'm just being me. I am who I am. I embrace you as a person and I got nothing against you. I take no offense to what you do, but I couldn't help but wonder. I can't make you like or accept me. You can get with this or that. Bad attitudes are whack! I'm contagious to those kinds of behaviors. Positive vibes only in this atmosphere. Nobody is chasing you or begging you for approval. All I want is mutual respect. Enough of the shenanigans already! I'm always coming and going, so if we happen to meet again, let's have a little talk and set the record straight. It's time for a new narrative!

# HUMILIATION

By Aaron Woodson

It's Christmas Day, and this is the saddest and most difficult time of the year for me. Just about every Christmas it's always been this way! This Christmas hits a little different than ones in the past. Christmas is supposed to be about giving and receiving gifts. This year I received the gift of humiliation. In my heart where there is usually happiness and contentment, these emotions have now been replaced with frustration, resentment, and shame. I can take responsibility for some of the things I may have brought upon myself, but there were some contributing factors that led to this! There was a situation that resulted in a separation. Lack of communication and empathy brought about a tragic end. I thought our love was pure magic, but instead everything went up in smoke! The loss is definitely causing me suffocating anxiety! We were planning a wedding celebration, but it just wasn't meant to be. The plug was definitely pulled from this relationship. Unfortunately, it's very sad. I was excited and proud to make you my wife, but then you decided to become irrational! None of this makes any practical sense to me. The notification of our expiration date blindsided me, so of course we had a confrontation. I told all my close friends and family that you were the one, but you turned out to be a mistake! This heartbreak is like a soundtrack that will play over and over again! I'm trying to shake off this funk, but right now I'm singing the blues. This isn't an exaggeration. Like Jay-Z, I can't see them coming down my eyes, so I gotta let the poem cry. There has been a wound that was exposed to infection. I'm not trying to put a Band-Aid over my pain. I just need time to heal. I recognize what's real. I can't let this shit steal my joy! I speak butterfly language, but these caterpillars don't comprehend it. I'm in my cocoon, my bubble of space. I occupy the space until I'm ready to break out. I can't wait to fly above these circumstances and show off my latest transformation. My humiliation will only serve as a footnote in history. God will use my broken pieces to make me whole again! Jesus was humiliated, too, and His body was broken for us. He rose again and left us with a beautiful gift... the Holy Spirit! Just remember there is beauty in ashes.

# RESTING BITCH FACE

By Aaron Woodson

I've noticed some women in public wear something called a "Resting Bitch Face"! It's defined as a woman who naturally looks mean when her face is expressionless, without meaning to. The resting bitch face is kind of similar to a poker face. As guys we try to be observant when we decide whether or not to approach a beautiful woman. Sometimes the Resting Bitch Face will deter us from actually making a move. I'll just say this, guys: women are not going to make it easy for us. Most women want to present themselves as a "challenge," or they may be having a great time being alone or enjoying the company of their girlfriends! Despite her Resting Bitch Face, go show some confidence and just talk to her! The worst she can say is no! Don't be a beta, be an alpha! Although a Resting Bitch Face can seem intimidating, don't let it stop you from shooting your shot. Break through the barrier of the Resting Bitch Face. You got this!

*God & Self-Improvement*

# DEAD TO THE WORLD

By Aaron Woodson

When I look around and observe my surroundings, I see many different things happening. I have witnessed the good, the bad, and the ugly! This world just isn't full of sunshine and rainbows. There is evil, madness, and chaos that inhabit this place. However, I like to see the brighter side of things and also see the good in people. Human beings are judged and criticized for almost everything. Most people have become very sensitive to certain things. But what's even more alarming now is how we ignore or become desensitized to things that affect us. Ever since technology has been introduced, we've been distracted. Blind ambitions, agendas, money, and schemes. Our ears are covered by headphones. We're blocking out the world... it's like we don't want to see or hear anybody these days. Conversations are spent talking to the air or even a wall in this generation. Some of us can't even cope, that's why we turn to dope. Been going down the slippery slope for a while now. There's got to be hope for us who are dead to the world!

# BRIGHT SIDE

By Aaron Woodson

After lurking in the dark for so long, you begin to try to look on the bright side of things, trying to look for a light at the end of the tunnel. Hope and faith continue to spur you on in this journey of life, but what if the light you're looking for is actually embedded inside of you? Sometimes it may be hard to see or believe, but just know that it does exist! The world will try to dim your light if you let it! Stars in the sky still shine even though they are in the dark! Pictures still develop after they have been in the dark room! I've learned that, even in my own darkest times, Jesus does some of His best work in the dark! Darkness keeps things hidden, but what's done in the dark eventually gets exposed to the light! Looking on the bright side of things is indeed a revelation. It's a blessing to elevate beyond the valley of your circumstances. Most of us hope to get to heaven someday, but sometimes we don't realize we have heaven inside of us! When I look on the bright side, I have to look within! You should too! There will be brighter days my friends when you just look on the bright side.

# BABIES THAT LEARNED HOW TO LOVE

By Aaron Woodson

When babies fall down, we cheer them on and encourage them to keep trying to walk. We may even help pick them up when they fall sometimes. When they are able to finally balance themselves on two feet, their legs kind of wobble. When they are stabilized, they begin to take their first step. Then afterward they begin to take more steps. Before you know it they are walking, and then suddenly they start to run. As adults, when we fall, it's rare that we have anyone to help us. Most of the time we are left trying to do almost everything by ourselves. Sometimes we fall in life. That's OK, except we just can't allow ourselves to stay fallen. At some points in our lives we have to get back up again. It's OK to ask for help, but before you do, try to do everything you can to help yourself first. Babies are like sponges; they absorb almost everything. They observe us. They are full of life. They are absolutely precious human beings. We as adults are precious human beings too! Don't ever forget that! Babies need nourishment and so do we. Babies drink milk. Adults eat solid food. Babies need love and so do we. Everyone needs love... not one person is exempt. God's love is so great for us that He wants to be in our lives. He wants to be in our lives. He wants to spend time with His children. He smiles down on every one of us! He is pleased that He created us. He is our Father, and there will never be anything that separates us from His everlasting love. Give your babies hugs and kisses. Tell them you love them. Husbands and wives, give each other hugs and kisses too. Girlfriends and boyfriends, same thing. Family and friends, greet each other with open arms and show love to one another. And lastly, love your enemies too! Love is required and most desired in this world. Babies grow because of love, and we as grownups do too! When we get boo-boos or get scratched up, let's patch ourselves up. We may have our scars, but love will always heal our wounds. We all were once babies that have now learned how to love.

# PLAY YOUR POSITION

### By Aaron Woodson

In life we are given key roles or responsibilities. We have our abilities, capabilities, and weaknesses. We all have a role to play in this big jigsaw puzzle. Not everything will always be a natural fit for you! At some point you have to get out of your comfort zone, and at other times you just have to play your position no matter how hard or uncomfortable it may be. There are no guarantees... things will always change, even if it's your position. Whatever position you play make sure you're the best at it! Know your assignment and keep working diligently! Everything you're working for will pay off one day. Until then, play your position!

# RISK-TAKER

## By Aaron Woodson

I took a risk—actually I've taken many risks in my life. Most of the time I knew what I was getting myself into. I was confident, believing I had nothing to lose. Risks can be rewarding or they can be disappointing. You never know until you go for it! It's better to have tried and failed than to not ever have tried at all!
Or you can come out on the better side of things and feel like you're on top of the world. Risks come with investment. It's a chance to bet on yourself. No matter what odds you face, there is a chance of hope that you will prevail. A risk is nothing more than putting down a "good faith" deposit! Risks don't come with guarantees. I see them as nothing more than confidence builders. It is an opportunity for growth and improvement!

Coming up short doesn't mean you're a loser. All it means is you didn't get what you wanted this time... doesn't mean you won't ever get it because someday you possibly will. You'll risk putting yourself out there; just try it over and over again! Or maybe you just think it's not worth it. My friends, something worth having is worth fighting for!

Don't you dare quit. You are worth it. You owe it to yourself to try your best! You will overcome because you're an overcomer! I don't care what they say... you're better than that! I'm better than that! We're not defeated... we are capable and we will keep pushing forward. Some things require training. Training is a process. When you train you will face challenges. We must prepare for them and seek them out. Don't be afraid. "WE GOT THIS!"

For every level you want to ascend to, keep in mind that it requires you to be a better version of yourself to get there! So go out there and show the world what you're made of. We made it too far to quit now! Take the risk... Hold on to that desire! Hold on to that last rope of hope. Hold on to your faith. Remember God took the ultimate risk and sacrificed His son, Jesus, to die for us! We all know what that means. If He took a risk on humanity, why don't we take the risk to live the best lives that He gave to us? Be a risk-taker!

# WHAT MY FATHERS MEAN TO ME

By Aaron Woodson

Whenever I look to the sky, I always wondered what it meant to be a father. I searched for my father, and for so long I felt lost without him. I endured and thought I was left abandoned. I realized that wasn't true at all. I knew in my heart I had a Father in heaven and a father on earth who both love me very dearly! I sincerely am grateful to have the greatest teachers in life I've ever known. I have grown into a man that both my LORD and my father would be so proud of today.

My father on earth, whom I call "Dad," is my mentor and friend. He is a fisherman and always has nice catches! You were always a great captain, Dad, and you ran a tight ship! If I were a fish, I know I was your biggest catch of the day. On May 6, 1983, that is when that fish was born! I knew I could always swim to you even when the waters of life became rough. I learned to be tough, but I became a bit more of a gentleman because of you. Your smile so full of joy was always so happy to see me. You didn't have your father (my grandfather) for long, yet I was so fortunate to have you twice as long.

I'm proud to be a Woodson and carry the name you gave to me. I hope that I did it justice just like you have. I watched you battle your afflictions... you sir, are a warrior. It's been said that we are twins... guess you could say I'm a chip off the old block. I'm made in God's image. I mirror you, but I also reflect my spiritual father who sits on the throne! Both of you mean everything to me. I love my fathers! You both truly have shown me what it means to be a father! One day I will be called a father just like you. I'll show my children what it really means to be a father!

# INFLUENCE

By Aaron Woodson

I want to be a person of influence. I want to change atmospheres and environments! I realize the person I am now and the person I need to become! Influence bridges the gap and crosses many boundaries. I know that I have the power to make a difference and change so many lives! Temperatures have to adjust to the thermostat! It's never the other way around! We all have an influence on someone in our lives whether positive or negative. To have influence you must have confidence. To have influence you must connect with people and let them know that you care. To have influence you must be authentic and build and maintain trust with people. To have influence you must personally develop yourself and exhibit leadership. To be honest, we have all been shaped by different influences that have made us who we are today. You can be under the influence of alcohol or drugs that can critically affect your well-being. You can have influence in an important staff meeting where decisions may have to be made! Positive influences can make an impact that improves the lives and attitudes of people around you. Negative influences are just the opposite. Credibility is currency for an influencer. You have to give value to receive value in return. I have had many influences who made me into who I am today! I was created to serve and love people, but I will also influence people to love Jesus, for He is the greatest influence in my life!

# THICK SKIN

## By Aaron Woodson

I have black skin that covers my entire body... I wear it with pride! I can't hide the person that I am. I hate to admit it, but I can be sensitive at times. So I know I have to get thick skin. It's so easy to get defensive and caught up in your feelings. I need to wear thick skin like an elephant or rhinoceros! People can have an arsenal of insults... doesn't mean you have to believe that they are true. Don't take everything so personally. Whatever people believe is what they perceive. What you believe about you is all that really matters. Believe in yourself, and if there is something you need to change, take action and fix it! Take criticism with a grain of salt. Don't get salty with anybody. Just be a seasoned person full of grace and maturity. Your skin is like armor... let words ricochet off of you like a pinball machine. You are built to take what's being thrown your way! I'm like an armored tank... the one that should be impenetrable. I learned you have to make yourself a hard target and never an easy one. Don't allow yourself to be exploited. Your skin is made to be thick, not soft. Just don't become abrasive from the elements. Absorb the substance of who you are. You are a force that is unstoppable. Sometimes skin has to peel in order to reveal new skin. It's time to grow some thick skin! I'm wearing it from this moment on. I'm glad to embrace my new thick skin!

# EPIPHANY

By Aaron Woodson

I thought I left the past behind, but somehow it caught up to me like a sprinter in a marathon! I thought I could sweep it all under the rug and hope it would never appear again. But oh, how wrong could I be? Everything that's in the dark eventually come out in the light. The light always overpowers the darkness. I tried to hide behind my own shadow. I didn't want my pain and dirt to be exposed. We always think we can examine life by our own interpretations. Yet the funny thing is life examines us, especially in our hearts. Humanity likes to portray perfection. However, most of us don't like the reflection of our own imperfections. There needs to be a deeper introspection that subdues and brings us to humility. Egos are so frail and sensitive these days; so caught up in their reputation and not putting more emphasis on character! I admit, I was that guy. One day I had a divine encounter with Jesus. I was a captive to my sins, but He set me free. This has been my epiphany!

# INTERRUPTIONS

By Aaron Woodson

The world we live in is filled with so many interruptions. Sometimes it seems there is not enough time to pause. People love to talk but rarely take the time to listen. Conversations often get started and can get very interesting until the dreadful interruption. I believe people have short attention spans and want to be heard. I understand all that, except people have a tendency to blurt out whatever comes to mind without letting the other person finish what they have to say. Honestly, I don't think people intend to be rude when they are interrupting... it's just a very bad habit! Some of us are totally unaware of interrupting other people. Interruptions can be a total inconvenience—disturbing, too. There are interruptions that can be necessary to get someone's attention to give a warning, share important details, or respond to a situation. Sometimes interruptions can be opportunities to serve and be divine appointments. Plans get interrupted by unforeseen circumstances or people who genuinely need some kind of assistance. Interruptions can cause people to react in irritation, hostility, flexibility, or compassion. However, interruptions don't deter God; after all God is an Interrupter. He is not bound by time or death. Interruptions don't stand in God's way of His good work. God uses interruptions to show us His pursuing love for us. There is a ministry of interruptions that we are called to. Instead of seeing people as an interruption, see them as your ministry. Embrace interruptions because there could be a blessing behind them!

# DEALING WITH MYSELF

By Aaron Woodson

Every day I wake up and I have to deal with myself. I'm looking at the mirror and wondering if I even like the man in the mirror. I'm faced with choices and making tough decisions. These things not only affect me but others as well. I don't have all the answers, but I do have questions. Sometimes I feel stupid for even asking them. I just wish I knew everything already, so I have to continue learning. I feel overwhelmed at times, like I am just doing my best to keep it together. There are times I can become unglued. I admit I have my flaws. Still I find myself clawing and scratching to get back up and make it to the top! Life can be a slippery slope; there are times you will fall. Sometimes you just want to give up but know that you can't ever allow yourself to do that! I've taken many hits and blows. I do my best to take life's biggest punch! I'm a gladiator, but I can also be a weakling. I'm grown, yet I can't do this journey alone! I have to call out for help. I have to cry out in the name of Jesus. He knows me better than I know myself. There is no shame, guilt, or condemnation in His presence... ONLY LOVE, SPIRIT, and TRUTH! I am broken, but with Him I am whole! I'm still a work in progress... just a reminder to myself, I'm free and no longer bound to any chain that kept me in bondage. The way God deals with me is beyond what I can do for myself. Thank you, LORD!

# SPEAKING MY PIECE

### By Aaron Woodson

You see me for the amount of selfies I may take. I admit it may be a bit too much, but is it asking too much for people to care or even notice? I guess who I am scares you off. I wouldn't expect you to understand. I'm not perfect by any means. You see my flaws, yet you can't see my heart. I have good intentions, yet you seem disillusioned by what you see on the surface.

What is it about me you can't seem to embrace? I try to face each new day with an optimistic and positive outlook. I've taken my lumps, but now I'd rather take a lump of cash than continue getting bashed! There is a dash between our birth date and eventual death date. I wonder what people honestly would say at my funeral. Would they even bother to come?

When I'm absent from the body, I'll be present with the LORD. I look forward to my trip to heaven, but for now I will continue to endure. I will continue to run my race. I will continue to live my life for Christ. I'll decrease so that He may increase. Life is hard, but I know that I can do all things through Him that strengthens me. I consider everything pure joy. I'm still here. I'm still breathing. I'm still blessed. So therefore, I must be winning. Like me or not... I'm meant to be here! I have a purpose, and I shall fulfill it! I've spoken my piece!

# LITTLE BOY

By Aaron Woodson

Inside every man is a little boy crying for attention, a little boy that is in pain and needs to be lifted up. Although I'm no longer a child, I've grown into a man that still has the innocence of a child inside. Sometimes I just want to hide and be sheltered from this cold, cruel world. I've made my share of mistakes. I have my flaws. I try and save face by being courageous enough to keep enduring what life throws at me. I'm not a coward by any means. I'll stand and fight, but every now and then you sometimes get weary. I have come too far to give up now. I won't faint! All I'm asking for is that you have some compassion. Humanity needs more empathy. Most people are oblivious to their surroundings. They may see a child hurting and won't think twice about coming to their rescue. When you become an adult, I guess you don't require any more care or concern. Why do we have to wait until tragedy comes to shed tears? I would shed many tears for you, but I know you wouldn't even shed one tear for me. If the little boy inside me is crying, why can't you just be there and cry with me? It's OK, though; I know my tears aren't completely wasted. God counts every last one of them and He made sure to rescue me! You know why? Because He loves the little boy who's crying out for Him! And He loves all the other little boys crying out for Him too!

# A DEMONSTRATION OF LOVE

## By Aaron Woodson

Sometimes you just have to let people love you. They may not love you the way you want to be loved, but they love you in their own way. There has to be a demonstration of love for it to be effectively received. We are quite capable of loving ourselves and others on our own, so why do we desperately need the love of others? It's because we were taught what love looked like on the surface. What we didn't know is that love takes on many forms. Not only does love need to be demonstrated, it also needs to be communicated. Love is all around us, yet it can seem so distant or foreign to us. When love meets you where you are, it's the most beautiful and exciting experience ever! Love greets us all with a very warm welcome. How do we greet love in return? The best illustration of love was Jesus being crucified on the Cross of Calvary. Out of love He sacrificed His body for our sins to be redeemed. He paid the ultimate price. He loved us so much that He wanted us to be a part of His Holy Family! He loved us so much that He sent a Comforter, His Holy Spirit, to dwell within us! Even in His agony and pain, He forgave His enemies. He loved us even when we were still in sin! Love is the way. Love is the life. Love is the truth. Love heals; just be patient. Love remains ever hopeful. Love always endures. Love can't be forced into anything, and it has no fear! God loved us where we were. He loved us through it all. He will always love us, but in return we must love Him back! Whatever we give Him in love, He will respond to even greater with His love! We are made whole in His love!

# KEEP THAT SAME ENERGY

By Aaron Woodson

When I burst onto the scene, I came into this space that was surrounded by vibrant energy! The world is made up of molecules of energy that circulate into our everyday lives. Some energy is contagious, and we simply can't get enough of it. We want that reoccurring euphoric vibration over and over again. But there are other types of negative energy that don't translate well with most of us. It kind of rubs us the wrong way and sometimes you get a bad reaction to it. Or you can simply not invite that energy into your space.

The more I live, the more I realize that energy itself is a balance. Energy has levels. It can be collected, released, transferred, delayed, or even stopped. Positive vibes produce a good manifestation to not let negativity of any kind disturb your inner peace. Energy exists in the natural and in the supernatural. Energy can remain dormant or be exercised. The challenge we have with energy is how long we can sustain it a high level without overextending ourselves. At certain periods of our lives, we need to take time to rest. During that time we can recharge ourselves and build up our energy again to make it through another day! Let's pace ourselves! Energy is so critical to life... we could not exist without it.

On another note, I want to shift to another subject for a moment. I notice that individuals for whatever reason like to slander, condemn, criticize, demonize, judge, attack, vilify, and disparage a person's alleged behavior or character. Without any tangible evidence, people question and accuse a person or a group or people while neglecting the facts!

However, they'll give other people who do the same thing a free pass, better known as the benefit of the doubt. That's why I say keep the same energy all the way around! Let's keep it fair across the board! Take a stance and don't switch up just because you feel peer pressure to change your opinion. It's not cool to go from hot to cold... lukewarm is even worse! When you see me, my energy will be consistently the same. So, hopefully when you see me, you'll make sure you keep that same energy!

# NO MORE RIVALRIES

By Aaron Woodson

In sports you have rivalries. You find them in politics, companies, friendships, and even in families. My question is how are rivalries even born to begin with? Every person on this earth is blessed with special gifts or abilities. But sometimes envy and jealousy come creeping in and starts a competition between individuals. This becomes a battle for superiority, which can cause some serious bad blood! Some people will go to great lengths for popularity. People are constantly jockeying for position to get ahead! It's a sad state of affairs when it comes down to a new low of pettiness. C'mon, we are so much better than this. Instead of trying to one-up each other... how about we level up and empower each other! We should want the best for others as much as we want the best for ourselves. We can win and achieve so much more together than by having our own personal agendas! I believe that it's time to call a truce... putting our differences aside and focusing on the bigger picture. We gotta keep our eyes on the Scriptures. Remember we have an enemy. He is our biggest adversary, but we all know his demise will soon be at hand! Let us rejoice and move forward to a new beginning! NO MORE RIVALRIES!!!

# BALANCE

By Aaron Woodson

Learning just the right balance in life can be challenging. I find that BALANCE is so important and necessary in life, but sometimes things just don't stay balanced. It takes effort to keep things in order. Balance requires discipline. Balance requires preparation. To achieve balance, one must be intentional. Balance requires discernment. Balance requires stability. Balance requires measurement.

Sometimes you get off balance... you stumble... or you can fall. Do we measure ourselves by the mistakes we make or by the progress we have made? I think to achieve an equal balance of that assessment, you must take inventory of yourself and give yourself some grace. Sometimes we can be much too hard on ourselves. Sometimes we don't have accountability for our actions either.

Balance is an understanding of our own limitations and capabilities. Balance keeps you centered. When you're in alignment, you will have balance. When you're weak, your balance will be off.

Especially when you lift weights in the gym and you keep bench-pressing until you reach muscle failure, one arm sometimes seems a little bit stronger than the other. The other arm is weaker and will shake to keep up with the stronger arm. Balance can be practiced and trained. Balance needs equality.

Don't confuse balance with comparison. Just remember to know where or what you're centered on. The best place I can ever be centered is my faith in God! If I try to center myself on anything else, I'm out of position and therefore imbalanced.

It's hard to get knocked off balance when you're low to the ground. When you're standing upright, you can get knocked off your position. What I'm trying to say is that when you kneel down in prayer... it's really difficult for anything to knock you off balance because you're centered in your sacred space. You are not easily moved... Prayer is a demonstration of balance and power. You draw strength from prayer. Faith is activated when you pray! Faith, love, and hope keep you in balance. If you're spiritually bankrupt, make a deposit to God and watch Him balance your life according to His will!

Power comes with great responsibility, but God's power is the demonstration of His great love for us. He requires a demonstration from us as well... He needs a demonstration of love from us to show what a covenant relationship with Him is truly like. A relationship has to have balance because if it doesn't it surely won't last. Balance is the key to WHOLENESS!

# INSPIRATION

## By Aaron Woodson

There is no point playing defense when you can be on offense! Got that mighty O...it more than compensates for the D I bring! I'm dedicated to winning, that's why I be grinnin'! Success make everybody heads be spinning... but takin' Ls makes you humble. Everybody gotta take a fall every now and then. Not many people wanna mumble about that, though! Pull yourself together, you ain't out the game yet... you're still DANGEROUS! Be courageous and be on your grind. Find your treasure in them scriptures... renew that mind and in time that blessing shall be revealed! Let Him be your inspiration!

# NEVER LOSE THAT SMILE

By Aaron Woodson

Has anyone seen my smile lately? Oh, there it is... I seem to have found it again. Maybe it was buried deep behind my frown. Our deepest sorrows can sometimes drown out our greatest joys if we let them. Thankfully, I had a few reminders to help restore my joy and peace.

First, God showed me where I was and told me who I am in Him. He reminded me of my identity during my crisis. I looked deep within to find the man who resides in my spirit. Secondly, I found someone who saw me walking along the loneliest of valleys. I met her at a place called the land of the weeping. I wasn't at my best, yet she showed me empathy and compassion. Looking into her eyes, I saw hope again. God used this woman to show me how much He loved me. The best part is she is one of the reasons I'm smiling again.

I found my smile in a new place called love and happiness. I discovered my joy, and now all I want to do is shout. I just want to sing. I just want to shout to the LORD and say, "Thank you, Jesus!" I will never lose that smile again. A smile belongs on my face. I deserve to show off my smile. People better get used to it because I'm gonna be happy. You should be happy too. The past has come and gone. The days and nights have come and gone. Now these three remain: hope, faith, and love. The greatest of these is love.

Love should be the reason we all smile. A smile shows confidence. It displays a calmness, says that you have triumphed and overcome. A smile is big like a giant... it can also be a sign of defiance or just resilience and maybe even a show of brilliance. No matter what, never lose that smile!

# GRUDGES

By Aaron Woodson

People hold grudges like they got a wedgie stuck up their ass! Excuse my graphic description, but I'm just being raw. It's a shame that people hold on to shit they should have let go of a long time ago. Relieve yourself from the burden of constipation. Don't let grudges be like a kidney stone... it will pass, but it sure will hurt like hell. Remove that toxic waste from your system. Forgive one another! Flush the grudge "turd" down the toilet. Wipe the stank off your ass, see how much better you'll feel! Life is too short to be holding grudges. You block your blessings like a blocked artery. Grudges are like blood clots. Don't be ashamed to apologize if you did someone wrong. If someone did you wrong, don't be so hard-hearted either! Grudges are like brick walls that won't budge. Stubborn pride leads to a downfall. Like the old saying goes, "A hard head makes a soft ass!" I'll admit, I've acted like a jackass one too many times in my life. I've held grudges, and I can tell you that shit don't feel good at all. Holding grudges doesn't do you any bit of good. You're only hurting yourself! We all have done a little wrong. It's time to stop dragging things out for so long. It's time to stop this shit once and for all. Listen, if I ever did you wrong in any kind of way, I'm very sorry, please forgive me! I'm working on being a better man. We can heal unresolved issues if we communicate properly to one another. When we know better, we tend to do much better. Bury those grudges like a dog burying a bone. Don't ever dig that shit up no more! It's done... LET IT GO!

# EXCUSES

By Aaron Woodson

The world is filled with so many people and excuses. We've all been guilty of giving them from time to time, including me. We often use excuses as an alibi or to justify something. Excuses are so easy to give, and most people just eat them up! For most people, excuses are just unacceptable! Excuses are like a pass most people want to use to avoid consequences or accountability. Excuses can get old very quickly, and they can be very annoying. I could write a book on the many excuses I've given. People don't want to take the blame for their actions and want to be seen in a favorable light! Admitting to your faults and taking responsibility builds character. Instead of passing the blame to someone else, take ownership! Hold yourself to a higher standard. Do it before someone else will. Excuses are unnecessary. Time and breath are wasted giving excuses. It's embarrassing and just disappointing. Do yourself a favor and don't be that person! Get out of that bad habit. I speak for myself too! With that said, no more excuses!

# TAKE ONE FOR THE TEAM

By Aaron Woodson

A team is defined as a group of individuals working together to achieve their goal. In life, you may have participated or been a part of various teams. Sometimes you may find yourself excluded from a team. You may have been overlooked, rejected, or simply not been asked to join the team. I've been on good teams, and I've been on some bad teams!

There is no "I" in team... it's all about "we." You have different backgrounds, different abilities, and different learning capacities! Together it is vital to the group's success that we mesh! For the sake of the goal, you put aside your egos and differences. Sometimes one guy on the team has to do the "dirty work" or the most undesirable thing most people don't want to do. Bottom line: sometimes you just have to take one for the team! On almost every team, you have an unsung hero who sacrifices to ensure the team's success. When a team meets and achieves their goal, it should be a great time to celebrate.

Some people can feel isolated or alienated to where they feel they're not part of the team. They may feel like they didn't do enough to contribute to the team's success. Or if the team loses or comes short of their goal, one or more individuals of that team may feel responsible for that loss or shortcoming. A team doesn't point fingers at one another and should never single anyone out! This is where we all should take one for the team! Embrace unity. Eliminate division!

# HE WILL CARRY ME THROUGH

By Aaron Woodson

There is no joy in emptiness or loneliness, so you have to look outside of them and see that there is something far greater beyond them. The world only brings death, pain, destruction, rage, and confusion, but Jesus brings life, hope, love, peace, and healing. Even though I have two legs and two feet, I still feel as though I'm hobbling along in this life. However, I thank God that He is my crutch! I can lean on Him or I can just kneel before Him! He knows what I go through. He sees it all even when everyone else is oblivious to it. I have to keep walking it out by faith, one day at a time, one step at a time. When I cannot take another step, He will carry me through, all the way home!

# MY ROAD TO DAMASCUS

## By Aaron Woodson

I waited and debated where I should go from here. Finally after being given much needed clarity, I see where I need to go! Like Paul, I was on the road to Damascus. After my encounter with God, He became my compass. He ordered my steps, and I found the stairway to heaven. I go boldly before the throne and give all my heart's desires to the King. I sing His praises all day long for what He brought me through. I once was blind, but now I see. He opened my eyes—after seeing one door close... behold, another one has opened! Thank you, Jesus!

# THE CROSS

## By Aaron Woodson

Every day I have a cross to bear. I'm not talking about wearing one. I'm talking about carrying one! I used to say I'd rather be judged by twelve than carried out by six, but my Jesus was nailed to a cross... all for our salvation. Love has always been my motivation, but having a family has always been His. I've been hustling every day since Day One. God created this whole universe way before me. He gave me all I need, yet I'm still wanting more. I don't mean to seem greedy... like the poor, I'm just needy. Today my pockets say I'm broke as hell, but tomorrow I'll get rich or die trying! Or maybe I'll just keep walking it out. Another day above ground is a good day. The day I ascend with the LORD will be an even greater day! The cross was a symbol of suffering, but it was necessary for our freedom from sin. No longer are we slaves to sin, but now we are heirs to the King of all Kings! Thank God for the cross. Let it be a reminder for what was and is to come He shall return... let us get ready! The King is on His way back to bring His kingdom on earth! The cross was never meant to hold Him. He rose again to be reunited with His Father. We are reconciled horizontally and vertically to Him just like the cross!

# HUMAN TRAFFICKING

By Aaron Woodson

Cruisin' these streets, rollin' past these busy intersections. So much activity is happening. What's really going on? Let me tell you what it really is. I see traffic, but I'm also seeing real-life human trafficking in my own city. I thought this kind of thing only happened overseas, and now I see it's going on in our own backyard. Beautiful, tortured, tormented, abused, hurt women being forced to do illegal activities by cowardly so-called pimps. It's a very sad scene how these men use these women to seduce other men. What a horrible and vicious cycle. This is modern-day slavery. These women are trying to make a living, yet they are being exploited and taken advantage of. I guess it's all about the hustle for them, but they don't realize they are victims of predatory schemes. They don't know their worth. If only they knew their true value, they could see they are precious jewels to this world! They are diamonds in the rough, covered in the vomit of sin. I really pray for them and believe there is hope for the lost. By no means am I judging them... I just have sympathy for them. Even God can use a prostitute, just ask Rahab! Like motivational speaker Trent Shelton would say, "It's rehab time!" There is a cure for the disease of ratchedness... I suggest a recommended prescription of righteousness. Jesus saves and heals the sick! He loves the sinner but hates the sin! I believe in the miracle of healing and restoration. Keep your head up, ladies that are caught up in the trafficking intersection. God will pave a new road for you to continue your walk. Receive it right now. Amen!

# THE BLESSING IS IN THE WRESTLING

By Aaron Woodson

As a child, I loved to watch wrestling. I enjoyed seeing my favorite wrestlers like Hulk Hogan, The Undertaker, Bret Hart, Macho Man, Honky Tonk Man, and The Ultimate Warrior put on a great show for fans like me. I used to think that wrestling was real until I came to a sad realization that it was fake! It was all a show just to entertain viewers. Even though it was fake, it always seemed real to me. It felt like the wrestlers that get into the ring to do battle with each other were telling a story. Each wrestler had their own finishing move that they executed to perfection. The finishing move would render their opponent incapacitated, and they would pin them to get the victory. In the Word of God it says that we don't just wrestle against flesh and blood but against spiritual principalities and dark forces of this world. Jacob, the son of Joseph, wrestled the angel of the LORD. Jacob wrestled with him all night and he didn't give up. He wouldn't stop wrestling with the angel of the LORD until he blessed him. In life, we all are wrestling or battling with something. I just want to encourage you to keep on wrestling. Don't give up because the blessing is in the wrestling. We all have to go through something to get something. Just remember the battle that you're fighting is not yours... it's the LORD's. Remember, the blessing is always in the wrestling!

# FACE YOURSELF

By Aaron Woodson

The sun rises and sets, yet it plays peek-a-boo. The sky sometimes hides behind a fleet of clouds. Rain is hidden inside them to pour out onto a world crying out for some much-needed attention. Nonetheless, all these elements seem to appear and then disappear. All of this is controlled by Our Maker... He is the One who orchestrates this whole show.

Have you ever just wanted to go run and hide somewhere? Ask Adam and Eve about how that worked out for them. They hid from God out of fear because they knew they committed a sin of disobedience. They told God they were naked. God gave them clothes and drove them out of the beautiful environment of Eden. Apparently most of the human race is uncomfortable with transparency and accountability. Sometimes we hide or try to escape from wounds or hurts that have been inflicted upon us. We want to protect ourselves from the daggers of harm... our pain is bleeding out from hearts and souls.

It seems unbearable until you realize you can eventually heal from it. Or you hide because you know you have done wrong and don't want to deal with the consequences of your actions. So if I hid my face, would I be considered a coward? If you hid your face, would you be considered the same? Hiding is a defense mechanism, but it brings you into the uncharted territory of isolation.

When we hide, we are demonstrating fear or shame. Not everyone knows how to deal with confrontation properly. We all were made to be more than conquerors! What do we have to fear? Even if we are a little afraid... just remember even Jesus was a little afraid, too, before

His crucifixion. In the face of fear, He still did what He had to do all because of His immeasurable love for us! Could we really face our worst fears? Sure we can! Perfect love casts out all fear!

What is meant to be seen and what is meant not to be seen? Even in the event of our humiliation and shame, God still gets the glory! Many times, I've wanted to hide. Actually, I did hide! Hiding is comfortable and can be a natural reaction. I can tell you this... hiding never gave me victory! I was never meant to hide. People always can spot me, and I'm easily recognizable.

Like David, I refuse to hide from my giants. I will face them with courage, and I will show my face in the name of Jesus. I am anointed, and my face shall be like Moses's transfiguration when he met with God. When you see me, my face will no longer be hidden... I finally learned to have the courage to face myself!

# MAKE IT STOP

By Aaron Woodson

What I'm witnessing before my eyes makes me want to erupt like a volcano. School shootings are happening at an alarming rate. Kids meet their terrible fate way too soon. I'm tired of these kids killing each other. Nowadays, these kids trying to act so tough, thinking that they got it so rough. I'm about to pull their card. You got it so good, but you're so damn ungrateful. Parents do the best they can to raise you up, but you got no respect for anyone... not even for yourself. You're quick to wanna blame and pull that trigger... y'all ain't nothing but cowards that need some sense knocked into you! That was how they did it in the old school. You come from the school of hard knocks, trying to sell rocks. You think it's cool to shoot up schools and break all the rules, acting like a bunch of damn fools. Need to get y'all minds right, get in them books, and learn something. Don't you wanna be somebody when you grow up? You wanna be cool 'cause you think it's gangsta to carry a gun... but taking lives that matter ain't cool! Don't you care about anybody but your damn self? It's a different world out in the streets. Nobody can rescue you from your own destruction. Fall in line and follow instructions... you are not above the law. Pull your pants up because I'm giving you the skinny on how to tighten it up! You're a bunch of kids, just babies... you're not killers! Y'all ain't really about that life. Quit causing all this unnecessary strife. Maybe one day you can live out your dreams of making it out of the gutter. Do the right thing, young men; put the guns down. Pick up a book and get knowledge. Follow God and keep Him first in your lives. Be wise, young men; let's all pray for a better way. Let's make it stop! Amen.

# THE DAWN OF ENLIGHTENMENT

### By Aaron Woodson

I never claimed to be the smartest guy in the world. There is so much I don't know. I'm still trying to learn and grow. Please forgive me of my ignorance; I come from the school of hard knocks. I'm still discovering my brilliance among the stars. We are all like constellations along the enchanting sky. Some of us are brighter than others, but no matter what, a star is still born a star! My time will come to illuminate the sky. I will even go as far as illuminating the hearts and minds of this world. Remember, one light can touch billions! Observe the candle... one single candle can light up all the other candles. Light can be shared. Warmth can be shared. And most certainly knowledge can be shared too. Dare to ask for wisdom and let it be paired with your moral compass: your heart. We will find our way and no longer be a lost generation! Let us enter into the Dawn of Enlightenment!

# A MATTER OF PRECIOUS TIME

By Aaron Woodson

All my life I wasn't quite content with the present. I've always desired that tomorrow would come sooner. I got tired of waiting and waiting and waiting! Oh, how I tried to live like there was no tomorrow. Trying to outrun time is impossible. Life is a marathon, not a sprint. I've been in the dark for so long, I sometimes forgot what the sun looked like. I feel like I'm racing against time faster than a heartbeat! There is so much to do in such little time. It's important that we value time and space. I'm trying to find my space in this world. I still have a pulse... I'm still alive... I still have a purpose! God brought me this far; now I have to take it further. We all got an expiration date, a date with death. That's the reward we all can look forward to. We can't escape it or run from it. Eventually it catches up to us. Time is undefeated. The sun retreats at the end of the day but comes back to rise again. Time leaves no void; it consumes our very existence. I've learned that time never cooperates with us; the best way to cooperate with time is through patience. A lot can be taught in such a time; wisdom speaks through the air to get our attention. We all have to make good use of our time; we can't afford to waste even a second. Time you will never get back. Time gives me hope. It gives me hope for a better tomorrow if it is promised! It's all a matter of precious time!

# LORD, BRING US BACK

By Aaron Woodson

People talking 'bout staying woke, yet my people stay broke. Y'all like, He didn't just go there, did he? Yeah, I took it there. I'm about to break it down to the masses. We live in a broken world, hell on earth, but we can look forward to getting to heaven someday. For what it's worth, life has given us a second chance. Why not make the most of it and run with it? So divided and double-minded we are as a people, we need to be reminded of The Way, The Life, and The Truth! We need to escape from this victim mentality that has us held prisoners. It's time that we set the captives free. We live in the land of the free, but everything in this world comes at a cost. Ask Jesus what it cost Him when He laid down His life for us sinners. By His grace we are saved. His love paved the way for all generations to know Him and embrace Him. Nobody is perfect, but we are made perfect in His image. Take a look in the mirror. Pause and reflect on what you see. You are not a mistake even though we make plenty of them. We can never be separated from His love. Most of us are hurt and in our feelings. It's OK because we are human, but just know you can cast all those burdens down at the foot of the cross. Know that every knee shall bow and every tongue must confess that He is Lord. Greater is He that is in you than He that is in the world. Don't let this world deceive you; know how your Creator perceives you. He loves us more than we can ever imagine. Nothing is too big for Him. Let Him be your strength and your shield. Let Him reign over your life... just surrender! Surrender to the name of Jesus. Lord, bring us back!

# THE OVERCOMER WHO IS REDEEMED

By Aaron Woodson

I was the kind of guy that people didn't expect much from. I was underrated. But one thing about me was you could never count me out! I got knocked down a few times, but like Rocky I always got back up! In this life I've been hit hard many times. I'm not the only one who has taken some punishment. Some of us have it worse than others, but I continued to fight and hit back even harder. Sometimes I felt like throwing in the towel, but I would urge myself to keep going strong! To tell you the truth, I didn't know how long I would last. Everything in life can happen so fast. I've stood on my own two feet, even if I was against the ropes. All of my failures and successes have been witnessed by the Man Upstairs. He always kept me encouraged through His Word and Holy Spirit. Growing up I didn't have many friends; the very few I did have either become frenemies or we just had to separate to elevate. I appreciate the good times I've had, even the bad times too. They were all lessons and blessings in disguise. I am thankful to have made it this far. I never would have made it without Him. He is the reason for my season! I am producing good fruit right now because I am connected to the True Vine! He nourishes my spirit. I had to get rid of the old wineskins because He's making me into new wine! I feel so fine now. He allowed me to sit at His table and sup with Him. I'm no stranger, but a welcomed guest. He sits me on high places and keeps a hedge of protection around me always. He is my fortress. I dwell in His house; He dwells within me. Like David said in Psalm 23, surely goodness and mercy will follow me all the days of my life!

# TIME'S UP

By Aaron Woodson

Men, they say our time is up! Our women are fed up with our behavior and actions that may be inappropriate. I will say oftentimes we do this by saying or doing foolish things. We make mistakes, and we are not perfect. However, we should also be held accountable. All women deserve so much better from us, but at the same time, so many men are labeled and under attack by women saying malicious things that emasculate our character. Men and women both deserve respect! We need to put some respect on each other's names. Discrimination isn't only geared toward women as victims, but it happens to men too! I get tired of some women that paint the picture of men as the bad guy. Not all of us are "bad men!" Some of y'all got some nerve. Most of you have had good men in your lives, but you treat them so poorly! Some of you ladies think you're entitled to a good man. How about learning how to be a good woman first! Men and women should be held to a higher standard when it comes to accountability. Men aren't always the ones to blame. Women aren't always the ones to blame either, but we do have a responsibility to treat others the way we want to be treated. Most of us men do share the blame or are willing to take ownership. So, ladies don't ever feel like you're alone because we are in this fight with you! It's time for us to break the cycle of feminism and misogynistic behavior should not be tolerated. Where did this battle of the sexes come from anyway? I believe I know that answer: it started in the Garden of Eden when sin was born into the world. Our genders should unite us, not divide us! Like the military, we should render all proper customs and courtesies. No pedestals are necessary, but together we can share a platform. Both genders can share the spotlight. Men and women shine brighter together when they are unified. Two is more powerful than one; there is strength in numbers!

Let's take a stand, not be on opposing sides. We can have a healthy debate. We won't always agree or see eye to eye. Stop with the third degree; we need to listen and communicate with each other! Let's be honest and respectful! We can hope for a positive outcome. Our children, siblings, family, friends, and partners look to us because we influence them. They need us to get it right. Equality can be achieved, yet love is the end result. Remember to love thy neighbor. May we do the work that is required to find harmony with each other. We still have time; let's heal the wounds that we have inflicted upon one another. It's time to call a truce; now isn't the time to refuse forgiveness! It's time to mend fences and stop wearing offenses like a T-shirt! If we are honest, we all have done dirt, so let's not pretend to skirt past our transgressions like we all innocent. The media has pushed the narrative for Time's Up and #MeToo. There are victims coming out claiming that they were abused. In some cases that could be true, but sometimes it's just lies at the end of the day! We all are broken people in a broken world. We have to make sure we find wholeness within ourselves. It's a process, but you can recover! One day our time will expire. When our time is up, it will really be up then, especially when God returns to bring His kingdom back to earth! TIME'S UP!

# CLOUT CHASER

By Aaron Woodson

I have no doubt in my mind that you're a clout chaser. You like to be around all the action and ride on the next person's coattails. You're living off of someone else's identity... why don't you make a name for yourself? All these idols you're chasing are doing you no good. You want to be associated with the so-called cool people or elites. You all about them labels, huh? So, tell me, what it is you're bringing to the table? You think you ridin' shotgun, but you all up in the back. Why can't you stand up for your own damn self? You just want attention and you stop at nothing at all costs! You already know what I'm about. I'm about my business, the kind of business that's called minding my own. I'm on my grown man shit, suit and tie shit. I'm making moves. I refuse to be a pawn in anyone else's silly little game. If you think I'm down for that, then you're dead wrong. I make investments, and I'm gonna keep it a buck wit' ya 'cause I'm down wit' ya! The way you keep going on this path, you're about to lose one, homie. I'm trying to school you to the game, but you seem to be about that hard knock life. Stop having your hands out. Ask God for what you need; He's got it all in abundance. Seek Him first, and all these things shall be added unto you. Remember, greater is He that is in you than he that is in the world. You were born for greatness. Don't settle for scraps. I don't need to get the strap, but believe I get it poppin'! All things eventually got to come to an end. You need to go back and find Jesus, my friend, 'cause He is the Only Way. I'm praying for you, man. Stay up!

# THE THRONE

## By Aaron Woodson

I stand at the door and knock, waiting for God's response. He tells me to come forth. I enter His sanctuary and humble myself before His throne. I fall to my knees and bow before His Majesty. My tongue confesses my sins to be forgiven. I thank Him for all the blessings He's allowed me to receive. Almost as if by instinct, I begin to pray and state what's on my heart. Like the servant I am, I reach to grab my LORD's feet. I cry out and ask for His gracious mercy. On the throne He sits on High. On the throne He reigns sovereign. On the throne, He is mighty and powerful. He is my Commander in Chief, and I will serve Him until I die. There is only One who sits on the throne, and He will rule forever and ever!

# PHOBIAS

By Aaron Woodson

I'm all alone, no land or sign of shore in sight. It's dark, and I'm in open space. I need help finding my way back. I'm lost. Can somebody help me? Anybody? Where are you? I'm afraid I will drown. I know what sinking to a new low feels like, but this could bring me down to the ocean floor of deep despair and isolation. I can't swim. Never been very good at it. I know I need to learn how, but I've made it this far in life without going in too deep. We all have our fears or phobias in life. It's completely normal and natural to feel afraid of something or someone. I think the real fear is when we lose control or don't know the outcome of a situation. Phobias are against the perceived threat of opposition. Fear retreats back into what is comfortable or safe. Fear is false evidence appearing real. I believe phobias present themselves as challenges for us to overcome. It's not always easy to conquer your fears, but it takes an incredible amount of courage and resolve to combat them. It is possible to triumph over your fears. It all starts with your mind. Anyone familiar with the fight, flight, or freeze method? Any time you're presented with a potential fear factor, you will more than likely be inclined to react in one of these three ways. Your body produces a chemical called adrenaline that will rapidly kick in and act as a defense mechanism to trigger you into action. For every action, there is a reaction. There are all kinds of phobias that we can all recognize. I can name a few that you may be all familiar with. We have claustrophobia (fear of closed places), agoraphobia (fear of open spaces), acrophobia (fear of high places), autophobia (fear of being alone), aerophobia (fear of flying), aquaphobia (fear of water), astraphobia (fear of storms, thunder, and lightning), pyrophobia (fear of fire), arachnophobia (fear of spiders), ophidiophobia (fear of snakes), philophobia (fear of falling in love), and homophobia (fear of

LGBT people). Phobias like these can cause extreme anxiety or panic for a person. Genetic and environmental factors can attribute to these problems as well. We as humans have exposure to different elements, places, and environments, so eventually we all are confronted with some of our worst phobias! Phobias can interfere with daily life. However, we can have power over them by having the courage to face them!

# ANXIETY

## By Aaron Woodson

I have a problem. I hate to admit it, but I have an issue with anxiety. If we are honest with ourselves, most of us battle with this crippling condition almost every single day of our lives. Anxiety is a mental health disorder. It can cause various symptoms that can affect your daily life. Feelings of worry, anxiety, or fear can bring on unnecessary stress and can attack our nerves. Having anxiety can be complicated and can cause serious tension. Anxiety brings on panic attacks and needs to be treated immediately. The environments we are in, the people we surround ourselves with, and circumstances we find ourselves in can greatly disrupt our daily functioning. Most of the time you may be able to recognize the symptoms, but other times you can't seem to figure out why you even have them. I can clearly identify that I have experienced agitation, restlessness, fatigue, difficulty concentrating, irritability, tense muscles, and trouble sleeping. Anxiety can be an overwhelming bout for anyone, but it can be overcome! As a man of faith, I know that I'm an overcomer. I want to share this scripture from Philippians 4:6-7. This may help you as it has helped me. "Do not be anxious about anything, but in every situation, by prayer and petition, with thanksgiving, present your requests to God. And the peace of God, which transcends all understanding, will guard your hearts and your minds in Christ Jesus."

# BREAKING BARRIERS

By Aaron Woodson

Every time I look in front of my path, there seems to be something standing in my way! Whatever it is seems to want to slow me down or stop me from getting where I need to be. I'm not about to be caught up in a tangled web and get stuck there! Life likes to present us all with challenges known as barriers. A barrier's job is to wear you down, discourage you, and make you doubt yourself. Whatever barriers may surround you, always remember you have the power to break barriers. On the other side of barriers is greatness. Don't allow barriers to block your blessings! The power of praise breaks barriers. Praise and prayer are rejuvenating. They break the yoke of bondage. The enemy will put barriers in your way so that you might stumble and feel defeated. It's OK to fall, but get back up and run through the obstacle. We all must adopt the mentality that we are unstoppable. You may break or fracture a bone attempting to go through a barrier. Remember, to work smarter and not harder, hurting yourself is not recommended. Barriers are lessons and you can definitely overcome them. Barriers come in many different forms. They come disguised as fear, doubt, worry, guilt, shame, anger, bitterness, unforgiveness, and so on. Barriers can also be a form of protection just like a football helmet! Buckle your chinstrap, keep your head down, but let your eyes be focused on your objective. Your breakthrough is beyond your barriers. When you meet your barriers, you'll certainly discover a breakthrough!

# TRANSITION

### By Aaron Woodson

I've been stuck on this island of stagnation for quite some time. It's time for me to do something about it. I'm ready to spark a change in my life. I refuse to sit on my ass and not do anything to better my situation. I refuse to be mediocre. I'm trying to expand my territory. Time for me to buy some acres and get some property to own. As long as I'm breathing and I got hands and feet, I'm going to use everything I have inside of me to succeed. Before you succeed, you must become familiar with the struggle. When you struggle, you have moments where things absolutely suck! You can't duck or avoid unfortunate circumstances for long; eventually it all catches up to you. Going from one place to another is called a transition. There are many modes of transportation in life. All of them will get you to your desired destination sooner or later. Some paths are fast or slow. Some paths are good and some are bad. In order to get transported anywhere, you must first be in position. If you're out of position, you will stumble, find yourself lost, and find yourself getting into trouble. After you get into position, you must start moving toward your objective or destination. Movement that is delayed or stopped for whatever reason can be perceived as procrastination, settling, or stagnation. Transition is all about making progress. Even if you struggle, you are making an effort to move forward. Transition is also a term relating to offense. In basketball, you have a point guard who sets the tempo of an offense, and he controls the floor. He sets up plays for his teammates to be in position for the best opportunity to score a basket. Do you follow me? Transition is never initiated when you're on defense. Transitions can also be considered "shifts." When you get in your vehicle, you have gears that you use to manipulate certain functions. We all have to park for an extended period of time.

I want to encourage us not to stay in park for a long period of time. You may become lazy, lethargic, or too comfortable there. Sometimes we have to go back in reverse to get out of a tight space, or we may have to step back in our lives and reevaluate certain aspects of a situation. We always want to be in Drive. This allows us to move ahead and navigate our roadmap through life. It is also important to have gas in the tank and have our foot on the gas to arrive at our respective destinations. All roads eventually meet and will reach a dead end. We will have our final transition from this earth to the afterlife. I have witnessed a loved one's final transition, and I'm sure some of you may have witnessed the same. I can tell you that it can be very sad because you may miss those that have departed. However, we also can celebrate what their lives offered us in the process. We all want to be remembered. Even Jesus wanted to be remembered. Birth transitioned us to life and life transitions us to death, but death transitions us to glorification!

# L.G.B.T. (LET GOD BRING TRUTH)

By Aaron Woodson

I have something to say to the LGBT community. You're not hated...you're loved! Not everyone has to necessarily agree with your lifestyle, but I believe it's time to look beyond what's on the surface. No matter what gender you prefer or prefer to be...you're still God's creation. No one has the right to discriminate, ridicule, or shame you for who you are. Let it be known that you're responsible for the life you choose to live. Lesbian, gay, bisexual, and transgender have a place in society. You are human before anything else. I know you're proud of your culture and you embrace it. There is Pride among you and you are proud to show your true colors. The rainbow comes naturally bent, doesn't mean it has to be bent to fit your agenda. Rainbows signals a promise that God himself only delivers! You are accepted and should be shown unconditional love and compassion. You can't seem to hide from your pride. God knows whose side your on. He doesn't condemn, but He doesn't tolerate an abomination of homosexuality. You're free to have your choice...however, every choice has benefits or consequences! May the truth set you free. Confusion contaminates warped minds and it isn't from God! It is all in His Word. Since you have a preference then you should be aware of the reference! Pride comes before the fall. Let Go and Be Transformed! (LGBT) LET GO AND LET GOD change your heart. Listen to His voice and draw near to Him. Turn away from what you do and let Him order your steps. He has a plan for each of our lives. Allow His Spirit to minister to you today. May the Holy Spirit break the yoke of bondage off you this very moment. Live in freedom in Christ! The name above all names. Be God-directed and not self-directed! Surrender to His will. He knows the road you're on will lead to your destruction. Please listen to His instruction. Resist the devil and flee. Open your eyes and see the truth for yourselves. Be delivered and come before Him. LGBT community LET GOD BRING TRUTH to you...don't dismiss what you know deep down is true!

# GIFT OF PRAISE

## By Aaron Woodson

The look in your eyes is like a sunrise. They glow like halos. I melt in the presence of your divinity, my angel of love! I pledge my allegiance to your love and glorious elegance. I almost passed up the chance to talk to you... so glad I came to my senses. You must understand that I've gone through life with foggy lenses at times. Baby, I realize now that you're the picture that makes everything so much clearer. I'm so happy that I can be your frame. Together we are God's perfect masterpieces. God's pure love encapsulates us; we are swallowed up in His wonderful grace and mercy. His face shines upon us and gives us peace! Let us wear smiles of joy and rejoice in His goodness. Love is more than a mood; it's a requirement! We are called to have discernment as we come to be under proper alignment. We are on a special assignment. Now may our beautiful union fulfill the prophecy that has been spoken over us, a prophetic word of blessing—let us receive it in the mighty name of Jesus. Masculinity, femininity, and humanity are all in the natural world, but divinity is supernatural. Together they become infinity but are subject to the Holy Trinity—the Father, the Son, and the Holy Spirit! There's no hierarchy, just one kingdom till He comes again! Let the heavens and angels sing as we receive our King! We love you, LORD; may You receive our gift of praise! Thank you, LORD!

# FOR THE WIDOWS

By Aaron Woodson

For every subject that's ever discussed, you rarely hear anything about the beloved widows. It's almost like they have been forgotten or lost in the conversation. There are many of them that exist, and a lot of them suffer in silence. Widows can often become reclusive and even a bit mysterious. Life can certainly be difficult for the widow. The love of their lives is gone; they are left to carry the burdens of their sorrow. Life goes on; there is a new reality they face on their own. Most widows just want to live a normal life, but losing their soul mate is abnormal. It's incomprehensible! It's not ideal; it's like it doesn't even feel real! It's like a piece of their puzzle is missing. Widows need support. They need love and encouragement. They need nourishment of tender affection and protection.

My late grandmothers became widows in this life; they gave more than they ever received. I know they had their moments to grieve, but no matter what they always believed God was with them! Widows learn more about themselves than they ever knew before; they do tasks that seem impossible. Coretta Scott King was a widow. Betty Shabazz was a widow. Jacqueline Kennedy Onassis was a widow. Priscilla Presley was a widow, just to name a few. These iconic women were wed to prolific and legendary men in history. They all carried their late husbands' legacies after they departed and keep their memories alive! It states in Psalm 68:5 that "Father of the fatherless and protector of the widow is God in His holy habitation." God values and loves the widow very much. In Psalm 146:9, "The Lord watches over the foreigner and sustains the fatherless and the widow, but he frustrates the ways of the wicked." Widows have a need to be cared for. They matter and should be properly loved and respected by the world. Let us watch over, protect, and love all widows. They are our neighbors, and we should love our neighbor as we love ourselves. God bless all of our widows! We love you.

# ROBBED

By Aaron Woodson

Have you ever been robbed of something that was a treasured possession? Many of us have had something or someone taken away from us without warning. The devil comes to steal, kill, and destroy. Most people lie, cheat, and steal from each other every day; someone becomes a victim and a price is always paid at the victim's expense. Robbery is an offense. Boundaries are violated. Lines are crossed when you are robbed. You understand me? I can share many stories in my life in which I've been robbed. I've had money stolen from me, personal items stolen from me, my career stolen from me, my joy temporarily stolen from me, and people I care about taken from me. All of those can be hard pills to digest... thieves can literally make you sick to your stomach! Losing your virginity robs you of your innocence and purity. Being raped definitely robs a survivor, at least for a time, of their peace of mind, dignity, and identity. You can even be robbed blind without knowing you're being taken for everything you have. Peace can be robbed from you in the blink of an eye. Opportunities can be robbed from you too. It's like having a rug swept out from under your feet. One of the worst feelings in the world is noticing you are missing something or someone! You may even feel emotionally or mentally bankrupt from the entire episode. It's quite traumatic, don't you think? There is no guarantee you'll even get back what you lost. You begin to feel like you're losing your senses and things start to become really tense! Robbery comes at an unfortunate cost to anyone's expense. When you're robbed you may even sob profusely over what has occurred. You may even get heated and want to avenge your loss. Being robbed strips you of your power and can lead you into the dangerous territory of hopelessness. But let me remind you of this: God restores tenfold! If He can restore Job, He can restore what has been robbed from you!

# SERVING GOD'S PEOPLE

By Aaron Woodson

The streets are filled with so much activity. Every day we drive past so many buildings, businesses, homes, and signs, but those who dwell in these areas are less fortunate or so-called misfits of society. We know them as the homeless, lost souls, drug addicts, drug dealers, pimps, and prostitutes. I see them and can't help but feel compassion for them! I don't pity them—there's a difference. It's easy to sit back and judge and poke fun at these people, yet none of us really can walk a mile in their shoes. Life can be tough, and we are only one step away from becoming one of them. Some of these people have been "cut off" from this world. God created all of us, including them too! We are called to love our neighbors as we love ourselves. Don't argue with me—it's in the Word of God! These beautiful people cry out for help; like the late Michael Jackson once said, "Who am I pretending not to see their need?" I guess we all need to remember to look at ourselves in the mirror. We need to change our ways of thinking. Nothing good comes from condemnation. We need a resolution. It's time for new solutions. There is so much pollution in this world. Not just the trash but the toxic waste, but we also need to rid ourselves of the toxicity in our minds. We have to remember that the earth we live on now is only a temporary residence. We are like strangers passing through. Technically, we are all homeless. At one time we all have felt hurt, lost, hopeless, had some addictions or abused substances, things, and people. We have to check ourselves before we talk about somebody else. It takes a community to rise up and care for each other in our neighborhoods! It's our responsibility to care for those who need rehabilitation and healing. I believe in the miraculous power of restoration and healing. Anything is possible with God. We are His vessels. We are created to do good works and show His glory to the world! If we say we love God, we must love our neighbors. We should be about our Father's business. His ministry is tending to His flock and caring for His sheep. We are empowered by His Word to go out and teach all nations the Gospel! People are suffering and are in need of Christ. If you don't have anything to give anyone, you can give them hope by praying for them. We need each other because we are one body in Christ! I love you all, my brothers and sisters!

# SELF-CARE

By Aaron Woodson

It's not selfish to take care of yourself. In fact, I encourage you to do some self-care. What good are you to others if you're not good to yourself? Too many times people neglect themselves to please or give to others. There is nothing wrong at all about caring about others, but putting people before yourself without any healthy boundaries is setting yourself up for disaster. YOU MATTER! You are just as important and valuable as anyone else walking the face of this earth. Don't ever forget that! Always treat yourself, don't cheat yourself! Self-care is rewarding and refreshing. Mental health should be taken seriously because it can adversely affect your quality of life. Never give anyone the power to affect your life in such a way that you are left defeated, discouraged, or depleted. Self-care is about taking responsibility and accountability for yourself. You're not meant to be put on a shelf. You are created and designed for a unique purpose. Own the platform that you are walking on. You stand firm on the foundations of your faith. Eliminate those doubts and just do! Like Yoda would say, there is either can or cannot; there is no try! It's OK to cry from time to time. It's healthy and necessary if it helps with your healing. Your brokenness will be restored to wholeness. You deserve to be happy. Be well and keep practicing self-care... you'll be so glad that you did!

# YOU MADE IT

By Aaron Woodson

Sometimes people will use, abuse, and misuse you. Sometimes people will even write you off. But that's OK, just dust yourself off and keep on moving! Don't let the haters stop your progress. Critics speak the loudest when they feel some type of way. Keep on going your way, pay no mind to what they say. You're a diamond, so continue to shine on! You've been cut, but that's what happens when you're built for greatness! Make sure all witness your powerful anointing! You have been through too much to let anyone stop your reign! It's time to exercise your authority. Make yourself the priority in spite of the majority! They need to put some respect on your name! This isn't about clout; it's about walking in your purpose. People love to talk but very few actually walk it out. Own your space. Not everyone can keep up at your pace, so run that race! Only you can run it the way you do! Go for it, go all out! Don't fall out, keep going! Leave them behind in your rearview. They have no choice but to fall back. They can't catch the blessings God is about to give you. What the enemy tried to use for bad, God turned around for your good! Rejoice when you face trials of various kinds. Let patience have her perfect work. Endure till the end and look forward to the day you hear the voice of God saying, "Well done, thy good and faithful servant!" You made it!

# MY JOURNEY: FROM THE MARATHON TO THE MOUNTAINTOP

By Aaron Woodson

Life is like a marathon, but I always seem to run it like a sprint. Sometimes I forget time is on my side. There ain't no rush. I just like to crush it daily, like the one that's caught my eye lately! Sometimes I'm afraid things will pass me by, so I've always moved in these streets a little bit different. I never want to be caught slippin'. I know I be trippin' sometimes, just trying to stay a few steps ahead of the game. God knows every move I'm going to make. He watches what I'm going to do. Even when I fall, He helps me get my focus back. I'm reminded that I lack for nothing; He supplies my every need. In my weakness, His grace is more than sufficient for me! I used to lean on my own understanding; I keep my eyes on Him and hear His voice much more clearly these days! He knows my heart's desires, but He requires me to follow Him and so that is exactly what I do! He is the vine, I'm the branch. Apart from Him I can do nothing. I know I'm nothing, but with Him in my life I'm everything. He's more to me than anything I'll ever need. He found me when I was lost. I'm on solid ground, and He takes me to high places. He loves me through all of the messes I've gotten myself into. He never left me or forsook me. I've climbed some hills, but He allowed me to see the mountaintop! The marathon continues with God, and I am now set free! I once was blind, but now I finally see. Thank you, God!

# ENCOURAGING WORDS FOR MY PEOPLE

By Aaron Woodson

We all were welcomed into this world, but once you live in it, you start to find out who is really for you. You won't always get a warm reception from people you encounter. People will look at you sideways from time to time. We live in a world of perception, and we often find ourselves in traps of deception. It's always good to receive the love and affection, but remember people will hate no matter what. Just keep it moving and stay on your grind. Hustle for your dreams. Don't let the crabs pull you into the bucket. Rise above the negativity. Flee from toxic environments—find someplace where you have room to grow. Pay special attention to detail. You are the head and not the tail. You have the power and dominion to trample over serpents and scorpions. God has put us on a new path and given us a new direction. Thank God for His wonderful protection. Look to God for inspiration because He always wants to show His demonstration of love for you! His Word nourishes and cleanses our spirits. Renew your mind, don't allow yourself to become blind to the truth. We are from the world, but we are not of this world. Man will fail you, but God never does and He never will. Stay in His will. Anything outside of it is truly no good for you! God has a plan for all of us. Abide in Him as He, too, will abide in you. Jesus was even persecuted, so don't think you're the only one that has to endure pain. We all have a cross to bear. Sometimes life can be very hard, but take heart. God is always with you, and He will always love you. Nothing you can do will ever change that. He is a constant friend, and He will never leave you nor forsake you. No weapon formed against you shall prosper. Keep walking it out in faith. Till we meet again.

# LEARNING CURVE

By Aaron Woodson

When you begin to try to learn something new, there is always a learning curve. Some of us are behind the eight ball. You can scratch a few times before you finally get the ball inside the pocket. Every game has a set of rules we all have to play by. If you stick to them you will have a good probability of success. You're not always guaranteed a great hand in life. You do the best you can with the cards you were given. You will make mistakes over and over again. I guess that's why they call them lessons. Limitations can hold you back if you let them. Overcome the odds that are against you and embrace the challenge. There is room to grow if you're willing to apply yourself. We are capable of learning at a high level. We are students in this classroom of life. We don't have it altogether, but we can start taking initiative and learn what we can for as long as we can. We can't allow ourselves to be mediocre. There must be evidence of proficiency and efficiency! Ignorance is a deficiency. Wisdom should have a permanent residency in our minds. Before we can get to experience great wisdom, we must first get through the learning curve.

# KISS FROM GOD

By Aaron Woodson

Have you ever waited for or anticipated a kiss? Some of us may have been so bold as to even plant one on someone without warning. Kisses are meant to be pleasant if they are welcomed. Kisses are public or private displays of affection. Kisses unlock the magic of intimacy. God kisses us in a much different way than we do. God kisses us when He blesses us! He kisses us when He answers our prayers. He kisses us when He comforts the brokenhearted. God kisses us when He wakes us up every day! Judas, one of Jesus's disciples, betrayed Him with a kiss. Jesus took that kiss of death, and He became the resurrected Savior. Then He met with the Father in heaven and kissed us all with the Holy Spirit! God will save the best kiss for last. If we are fortunate to make it into heaven to be with our Creator, He will bless us with our rewards. Living in eternity with God will be the greatest kiss we will ever witness. He is always faithful and true. I'm so thankful for my kiss from God! I love you, God, and thank you so much. Your kiss has saved me.

# FISHERS OF MEN (A FATHER & SON COLLABORATION)

By Robert J. Woodson and Aaron Woodson

(Father: Elder Robert J. Woodson)
I am a fisherman and a fisher of men,
Casting out to catch fish and trying to soul-win,
Either casting out a net or casting out a line,
Praying that I can be successful in catching fish for all time.
We probably all have had a day when a fish got away,
Keeping in mind that there is another day.

Some days you have your highs and on other days you have your lows, but I am always confident that my experience and techniques will grow. I have learned the technique of fishing for men and fishing for fish. I do not fish all year for fish but to win a soul for Christ each day is my only wish.

The weather does not permit me to fish for fish all year, I know.
Instead I am able to win souls for Christ wherever I go.
I can remember the days so vividly as a young lad when I went fishing with my dad. He showed me how to bait the hook and cast out the line and to wait patiently for the fish to bite and grab the pole when it was time.

It was the life experiences as a child on the fishing bank and the story of the Fisher of Men that made such an impact on my life over and over again. The world is in need of a Savior and for men to turn away from sin. We all must go into the highways and hedges and win souls for the kingdom.

(Son: Author Aaron T. Woodson)
I am like a big fish that came from a small pond. My humble beginnings started on the banks of Vallejo, California. At that time I was a young tadpole swimming along to find my way out. I propelled myself from the shallow waters into the deep. Sometimes I thought I was out of my element, but I learned to adapt and overcome! I've never been quite a fisherman like my dad, but I've found myself fishing for other things of my own in life. I've cast my line time and time again. Sometimes I have been successful in making a big catch and other times not so much.

Fishing is a sport and a skill. It requires patience, preparation, focus, and prayer. My mind will often wander to faraway places, when suddenly I feel a tugging on the fishing pole of my heart. I try to reel in what catches my eye while at the same time reeling in my emotions. I've had many delightful surprises and other times some disappointing moments. No matter the outcome, I am confident that my experience and techniques will grow.

I realized that I was fishing for just myself. One day I had a change of heart. I decided that I am now fishing for Christ. It's not about me, it's all about Jesus! In Philippians 3:7, it says, "But whatever gain I had, I counted as loss for the sake of Christ."

My dad was among the few who taught me to love God and know Him for myself. As a young boy, my dad took me fishing with him to a place called Lake Berryessa in Napa, California. It was a beautiful and private piece of property where people could go out and fish. My dad frequently went fishing there, and he became an expert fisherman.

He showed me how to fish and wait for the bite. We waited and waited till we could feel that tug on the line.

I remember we didn't catch anything that day, but I did learn a valuable lesson. Faith is the evidence of things not seen. Just because something doesn't happen at a particular time doesn't mean it will never happen. It's never our timing—it's always in Gods wonderful timing!

In the Word of God, Peter was a fisherman and Jesus helped him to become a fisher of men along with His other disciples. Instead of catching fish, Peter was catching and winning souls for Christ.

Life experiences transformed my life and made a lasting impact on me. Like my dad said, "We all must go into the highways and hedges and win souls for the kingdom." That's exactly what we are doing because we have become fishers of men!

*Emcee Battles*

# RESPECT IT

### By Aaron Woodson

Respect the mic... Respect the Hustle... put some respect on my name! I'm not about clout, just trying to cement my legacy. I've paid my dues to get to where I am. Oh, please believe it! Keep your mouth closed until you've walked a few miles in my shoes. It's easy to sit back and be a spectator. If you really want to take it further, just step into the arena. We can get this match started like American Gladiators. I'm coming out a winner. Take your L and go home! You're not on my level; polish up your game. Stay sharp! So, while you're working on that, I'll be over here being great. Respect it!

# ALL UP IN YOUR SPACE

By Aaron Woodson

I belong here, but I'm not welcomed in your space. This world seems overcrowded, yet we still have all this unoccupied space. All these faces of different races and color give a whole new meaning to diversity. Somehow people of various backgrounds have been categorized or put into these special groups to cause separation. We were meant to be integrated, not segregated. Equality has become something of an anomaly; there is a puzzle with many pieces, yet they don't quite fit together to make the big picture. Is there something missing here? We all are meant to share time and space. Restrictions and rules infringe upon the existence of our freedom and speech. Most people that belong to a particular race have been subjected to a certain degree of marginalization. We need to restructure our system's function: let's consider what is happening. This is nothing new; we all know what's going on like Marvin. There is a new threat or fear of globalization in the world today. It's time we direct our attention to mobilization and join forces. Maybe things will change course, but until then let's coexist. We all belong here, so please believe I ain't going nowhere until we all advance! I'm all up in your space!

# I CARRY WEIGHT

## By Aaron Woodson

I carry a lot of weight, straight tippin' the scales.
People can see it in plain sight.
I can't even lie, I'm over my limit.
People seem to notice every detail about my exterior.
But what they don't see is what's in my interior.

I carry a lot of weight.
I carry body weight, like I carry two in one.
I carry mental weight... my thoughts are heavy.
I carry emotional weight... I'm all bottled up with mixed emotions, my lid's about to pop off!
I carry spiritual weight, feels like the devil is trying to bring me down!

I know I'm a heavyweight. I was born to be in this weight class.
At this level, the adversity you face is much tougher.
Life can hit you in so many ways.
Sometimes it can catch you off guard and hit you below the belt.
No matter how hard you get hit or knocked down, you just have to keep fighting.

Boxing has rounds. Life has its moments. Everybody is watching.
All eyes are on you! Sometimes, I pull an okey-doke like the great Muhammad Ali.
When life has me against the ropes, I pretend I'm fine and just put on a show, but I'm really hurting on the inside.
I'm battling these demons of mine, and I know I will prevail against them.

But I can't do it alone. The Holy Spirit comes in and takes my place to put an end to the torture.
But like many battles we encounter, they eventually begin to take their toll.

The battle isn't mine; it's the LORD's!
I had to transfer all my excess weight over onto the altar.
Lay it all at His feet. It is there where I kneel and meet my Savior.
He knows my pain and hears my cries. I'm not ashamed to be who I am.

I was made by Him even if I am a heavyweight.
That's right, I believe I am a heavyweight. I got the strap to prove it.
Like Heavy D, the overweight lover is in the house.
Some of you ladies didn't like me when I was skinny, and some of you damn sure don't like me at this size.
But here's a newsflash: I don't give a shit because I'm secure within myself.

I'm too grown and sexy to ever let a broad get to me! I'm like Big Pun 'cause I hit you with the big gun, big ton!
My pockets will be on sumo, like Cube. I push rhymes like weight! I bring it to ya like FedEx Freight. I come ready to deliver! I CARRY WEIGHT!

# I'M THE MAN

By Aaron Woodson

I feel like I'm the man like Aloe Blacc. I play my position to win. And if I lose, I'm, like, let's run that back! For a long time I had to pick up the slack and tie up these loose ends. Been through a lot of rough patches... blood, sweat, and tears. Overcame my fears. Faced the man in the mirror and didn't even flinch. I told myself, I got this! I exude effervescent confidence. I'm not in any competition with any other brand but my own. Full grown like the beard on my face. I do my best to keep everything nice and trim. When I wrote my book, most people just skimmed through it. My words have meaning; they scream off the page. Each chapter in my life you turn to reads like a manuscript! I'm from the Bay, and ever since I left, I've felt like a fish out of water. Yet I found myself in a new pond, swimming along these banks of Jacksonville, Florida. Now I'm the fisherman, I've cast my line... baiting you all with my poetic rhymes! People trying to avoid the hook. Sooner or later, I'll grab your attention. One day they will mention me among all the greats! There won't be any debate that I was the man!

# JEALOUSY

## By Aaron Woodson

People have a tendency to think I'm overzealous, but perhaps they are really just jealous? Suspicion of my blessings arouses their attention. I sense the tension. Fake smiles disguised in deception. I stand at the podium of rejection. I know my audience has a certain perception of me. Did I mention I have a calm demeanor and a handsome complexion? I am a reflection of what they could only imagine. I'm ascending to a whole new dimension. I've made quite the impression. I'm sorry about your aggression and depression. May I suggest a way to cure your infections? Try a remedy of affection; it will ease your tensions. I hear your silent and sometimes loud objections, but here comes the gavel! You sit back and point fingers at me and judge. You like to put unnecessary labels on me that are unwarranted. You think you know me, but you don't even have a clue. Your obsession with me is quite excessive. Shouldn't you be more concerned with your own state of affairs? You have stones that you like to throw at me, but I took them and built a monument out of them. Thank you for helping me build a strong foundation. I still stand and deliver a barrage of powerful messages that will leave you in shock and awe! God is my witness. He is my Defender. He is my Protector. No weapon formed against me shall prosper. He fights my battles. Praise and prayer are my weapons against your jealousy. Your feud with me only sparks controversy. An end will be put to it, and we can finally put this matter to rest. Wishing you nothing but the best. I'll keep doing what I do best... and that's BEING GREAT!

# COMING OUT THE FRAME

By Aaron Woodson

All my life, all I wanted to do is win. I'm at the door, let me in! If not, I'll find my way into the building. Everybody, stand up, get your damn hands up! Pass me the mic, I got something to say. Pass me the plate, y'all been eatin' long enough! It's time for me to cut the cake! You gotta move... give me some room! I got the juice, I'm coming out the frame! This is the moment I've been waiting for. Ball's in my court now, I'm shootin' my shot. I bust every time. I'm out here breaking ankles, ask her why she got those cankles, though? I run the floor like Steph Curry. I stay on top of my game. I get off before the shot clock. Only she knows, I'm the real buzzer beater! She know I don't really need her... She play her position, but please believe she keeps coming back for more! I got no problem feedin' her some vitamin D! I'll make her see the rainbow like Skittles. I just might make her Starburst... having her feel all jolly like a Jolly Rancher. She feelin' herself, all Mushy Gushy! Aww suki suki now! I'm a Good fella but a BIG fella... I'm a force like a Roc-A-Fella! I rock the bells like Cool J. Mozart meets Humphrey Bogart, with this from-the-heart shit! I keep it J. Cole! Never lived a life of crime, but hating should definitely be an offense! I'm charging it to the game, though... Your time's up! Its game over, you Lil' Flips! None of you get the picture 'cause you don't have the frame of mind to be on my level. Nah, you can't be in the picture—you don't belong in it! Can't have greatness tainted... no spots or blemishes are acceptable. I relish the opportunity to outshine my opposition. You're a throwback, now you can just fall back! Let me get back to countin' my stacks! Find my books on the store racks... Face of Expression will be a best seller! That's how I frame it! I'm comin' out the frame!

# DON'T POKE THE BEAR

By Aaron Woodson

There is an old expression that people might want to beware of: "Don't poke the bear." I wouldn't take this warning lightly. Some people have a knack for getting on other people's nerves! They agitate, irritate, anger, or piss you off in the worst way. I deal with people like that sometimes, especially on the job. People have told me that I'm like a nice, big teddy bear. However, some people have never seen the other side of me! I can easily turn into a grizzly bear. I don't enjoy being poked or provoked by annoying people. I'm sure I've gotten on people's nerves too. I can honestly say it's never intentional or deliberate. For the most part I just try to stay in my own lane. I've given people fair warning at times not to poke the bear, yet they do it anyway. I can be kind, charming, and sweet until you meet Mr. Ferocious! I'm sure you have all dealt with many different personality types that have some issues with poking the bear. Sometimes you have to just leave it alone or let it go. If you poke the bear, you might hear a special kind of vocabulary that comes out of my mouth. I may want to even punch you in the face if pushed too far. So, if you're that person, just remember to stop poking the bear!

# RESPECT MY CALIBER

By Aaron Woodson

Giving and showing respect is like a foreign language to most people. They don't comprehend how to demonstrate it! People always seem comfortable to want you to tolerate their bullshit! I say, "Not today, Satan!" Off the rip, I'm not letting anything else slide. You ain't safe... you ain't safe! No more free passes! I think people need a curriculum on class. I guess some people think it's been dismissed. They never seem to get the lesson. They might learn better when they come face to face with the Smith and Wesson! You wanna pop off like a pistol? Be careful because you about to get pistol-whipped with some hard truth! I got plenty of bullets, and I ain't afraid to shoot off my arsenal! Being out of pocket should be a felony, but you know what? I'm gonna drop the charges on you this time! I could do some serious damage... don't think you gettin' off that easy. I'm still gonna teach you a lesson. I'm gonna teach you something about respect! You probably weren't expecting that, but oh, you gonna know about it! RESPECT MY CALIBER!

# HE DID IT

By Aaron Woodson

Greatness is imminent. I'm just trying to cement my legacy. I've mixed up all the ingredients of success and baked them up into a really nice cake. I'm like a candle: I stay lit! Gotta keep it shining bright. It took prayer and me being on my grind to produce these amazing results! Catapulted up to the sky, now I'm flying high! The heights I've reached don't know any boundaries. I've exchanged pleasantries with my past, present, and future. Guess you could say we're really acquainted. So now, watch this: I kissed my fears and insecurities goodbye. No more wondering why. Like Brian McKnight, I finally had my one last cry! Damn, this is beautiful! Now I know why I went through what I did to get here! This is my moment, get that red carpet out for me. Oh wait, I'm already on it! That's right, you better believe he did it!

# GENIUS IS COMMON

## By Aaron Woodson

My poetry is like photography, I capture all angles. Don't sleep on my genius. Remember, I do have a conscience! Life has many perspectives; sometimes we just need to focus and see things through a different lens. We need to have the vantage point of an eagle, see the vision clearer like 20/20! You can try to dissect my every word, but my message still won't make sense to most of y'all. If I'm not real to you, then you obviously can't even feel me. My words are packaged like Amazon. My pen delivers like UPS: Unparalleled Skill, Determined Will. Every day I'm killin' it! This is what it sounds like when a poet writes... when a poet writes his dopest poem! Oh, please believe his genius is common!

## About the Author

### *Aaron Woodson*

is a military veteran from Vallejo, California. At age of 15, he had a passion for poetry and began writing poems. He enlisted in the US Air Force in 2001 and served for 15 years. He had a vision to publish his very own work someday. The opportunity has finally come for the release of the highly anticipated book called Face of Expression. This is his first book that's ever been published. He has so much to offer  the world. The author is a very accomplished and interesting person. He is a former Security Forces Member, a casting & movie extra, enjoys fitness, traveling, dancing, singing, and writing poetry. He is single with no children.

www.ingramcontent.com/pod-product-compliance
Lightning Source LLC
Chambersburg PA
CBHW072013070526
44583CB00015B/1461